Decentralized Defense Against Volumetric DDoS

AF866033

By
David Laid

Table of Content

CHAPTER 1: INTRODUCTION

1.1 Distributed Denial of Service Attacks

Distributed Denial of Service Attacks (DDoS) is one of the Adverse Cyber Attacks that threaten the availability of the network, network resources, and network services from its legitimate users. Evolution in Computing power through cloud computing and Quantum computing as well as the availability of the internet has become one of the major factors in increasing DDoS attacks. In DDoS attacks, attackers disrupt the network and website operability by flooding a high volume of illegitimate requests, consuming the network resources like bandwidth, and server capacity which can lead to service disruption, poor website performance, and inaccessibility. Additionally, many DDoS attacks have been performed to gain the advantage of network disruption for backdoor access in a network, stealing confidential information, and performing other adverse cyber-attacks like data breaches, Network intrusion, malware distribution, social engineering attacks, etc.

In general, when DDoS attack overwhelms target server, attack traffic comes from diverse source of networks and machines (bots) which might be controlled by attacker in common scenarios with aimed to disrupt the availability of web-resources and services hosted on this target server. DDoS attack mainly harms the reputation of web services by either degrading the performance of service for normal user and at the end target would be crash the target server or completely shut down the target server by flooding massive amount of traffic pretends as a legitimate traffic. The conceptual scenario is depicted in Figure 1.1.

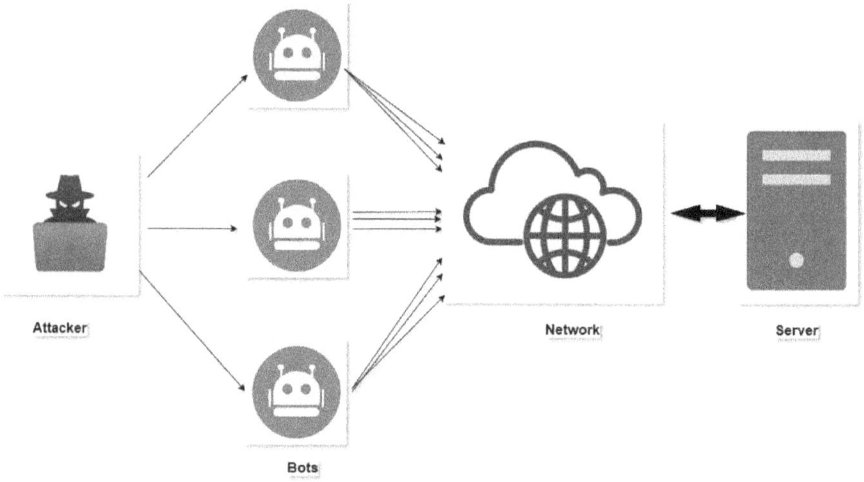

Figure 1.1 DDoS attack overwhelming a target network.

1.1.1. Types of DDoS Attacks

DDoS attacks are categorized based on the Attack Vectors and targeted Network (OSI) Layers:

1.1.1.1. DDoS attack types based on Attack Vectors:

A) Volumetric / Volume-based Attacks

Volumetric / Volume-based DDoS attack is type of DDoS attack where immense amount of traffic flood the webservers, network infrastructures and consume bandwidth of the network. Enormous volume of traffic is the distinct feature of these types of attacks over network infrastructure additionally; it is most destructive form of DDoS attacks. Main motive behind this attack to consume all available network bandwidth by flooding massive amount of traffic to overall network infrastructure. Intensity of Volume-based attack is basically measured in Packets per Second (pps) or Bits per second. Common examples of Volumetric attack are UDP flood, ICMP flood (Ping flood), TCP flood, DNS Amplification. And mainly Volumetric attacks targeted towards network layer and transport layer of OSI Model.

Common attack mitigation strategies involve use third-party cloud solutions, rate limiting, Ingress & Egress Filtering, utilize CDN to serve traffic, Deploy Hardware Firewalls & Access Control List (ACL), and Overprovisioning Bandwidth. Mainly mitigation performed either using network layer security devices or by replying on third-part cloud solutions.

B) Protocol Attacks

By exploiting some vulnerabilities present on the network protocols, protocol attacks are initiated towards network ecosystem and become reason for service disruption and network resource exhaustion. In this type of attack, attackers take advantage of existing protocol's behavior or its limitations to disrupt availability of the webserver or networking ecosystem. Protocol attacks mainly noticed at transport layer and application layer of system. Mainly protocol attacks consumes massive network resources, such as memory, CPU power, and connection pools, thread pools which ultimately leading to service disruption. SYN Flood, ACK Flood, DNS Amplification, NTP Amplification, Smurf Attack, Fragmentation Attack, TCP RST, HTTP Flood, BGP Hijacking are some common examples of Protocol attacks. Connection per Second (CPS), and Packets per Second are common measurement units of Protocol attacks.

while designing effective mitigate solution for Protocol attacks, by understanding behavior and vulnerability of implemented protocols are key consideration. Some common techniques are rate limiting, traffic analysis, cloud-based protections, Blackhole Routing, load balancing, and IP Blacklisting.

C) Application layer Attacks

By overwhelming application / system's resources such as CPU capacity, database connections pool, thread pool or memory, the end-user's application or functionality becomes the target of attackers. In this category of DDoS attack, end-user system / resources directly become victim of the DDoS attacks. Basically, measured in requests per second (RPS) and concurrent connections. In Application layer DDoS attacks, attackers generally flood the application with traffic by pretending it as it comes from legitimate sources, is one of the key characteristics of this attack. And it would become devastating as normal attack mitigation system identify the attack traffic as normal traffic because of this behavior, at the end availability of the system become compromised. Some common examples are HTTP Flood, Slowloris, Targeted API attacks, DNS query flood.

Web application firewall, Rate limiting, Content Delivery Network (CDN), traffic shaping, anomaly detection, Dynamic resource scaling, Bot Identification and mitigation, advanced packet sniffing tools, attack pattern identification tools are common examples of Application layer attacks. (Denial-of-Service Attack, 2025)

1.1.1.2. DDoS attack types based on Network (OSI) Model / layers:

A) Layer 7: Application Layer DDoS attacks

Top Layer of OSI Model, Application layer can be considered as a User Interface or a layer where user interact with system. It deals with representing data, information (in any format such as image, voice, text, video, live streaming data) to users in human-readable form and interact with lower layer, presentation layer, both layers are generally implemented together. In Layer 7: Application Layer DDoS attacks, attackers target the application, or end-user system by flooding / consuming resources of webservers where these applications are hosted as well as Databases and network resources which serve end-user application are also targeted. DDoS attack in this layer shares characteristics like Resource Exhaustion, targeting end-user applications and sometimes low volume of traffic to become undetectable under network security ecosystem.

Examples of Application Layer DDoS attacks are Slowloris, HTTP GET, HTTP POST, DNS query flood, SMTP flood. Application-level

Bot attack, VoIP (SIP) flood. Application layer DDoS attack Mitigation strategies involve deployment of Web Application Firewall (WAF), Rate limiting, implementing challenge/Response tests, use of Content Delivery System (CDN) to mainly to serve static content and load balancing.

B) Layer 6: Presentation Layer

Responsibility of Presentation layer are data encryption, decryption, compression, serialization, graphic commands, resolves data incompatibility issue of different operating systems and protocol conversation between different applications. Additionally, it also acts as middleman to transmit data between Application layer and its lower layers. DDoS attack surface of the presentation Layer is very minimal; it not directly handles request and response unlike other layers of OSI models. DDoS attack on Presentation layer is performed by using the cryptographic operations and techniques to flood network resources, consuming bandwidth and servers. By performing fake SSL/TLS handshake requests to SSL/TLS server, consuming the CPU and memory resources of servers (Encryption and decryption). Compression bomb, decompression bomb, SSL/TLS flood attack, Malformed Certificate Attacks, are some examples of Presentation layer DDoS attacks.

To mitigate of presentation layer DDoS attacks, implement various strategies and techniques such as Rate limiting, utilize load balancer, limiting decompression type and size, usage of validation of security certificates, implementing SYN cookies, usage of updated libraries, and enforce strict user validations. By implementing above strategies, we reduce the risk of Presentation layer DDoS attacks.

C) Layer 5: Session Layer

The Session layer responsible for creating interactive connection between two or more devices for specific period called session, managing sessions and terminating sessions. It also ensures that synchronization of data, session recovery and dialogue control. Remote procedure call (RPC), NetBIOS are practical examples of sessions. DDoS attack on Session layer involved Session Exhaustion Attack, Malformed Session Protocol Attacks, Telnet brute force attacks. Mainly stateful applications and services use sessions so DDoS attack surface commonly becomes session and session establishment mechanism. By implementing some common strategies such session timeout, Rate limiting to initiate session, usage of firewalls, deep packet inspection (DPI) and protocol validations, we reduce the risk of session layer DDoS attacks in our application ecosystem.

D) Layer 4: Transport Layer

Layer 4 of OSI model responsible for end-to-end communication of applications over a network, means transfer of data from application of source host to application of destination host over a network. It also watches over data transfer, reliability, and proper sequencing. Protocol used for transporting the data might be connection-oriented (TCP) or connectionless (UDP). DDoS attacks on Transport layer is mainly targeted these transportation protocols and flood the server and consuming network bandwidth and resources. Some common examples of Transport layer DDoS attacks are TCP SYN Flood, UDP Flood, TCP Reset Attack (RST Flood), De-synchronization attack.

Attack mitigation strategies involve Rate limiting, Deep Packet Inspection (DPI), Anomaly detection, implementation of firewalls and Access control lists (ACL), use of third-party scrubbing services, SYN Cookies, and TCP Proxying.

E) Layer 3: Network Layer

Network Layer is accountable for delivering packets across different networks, addressing routing, fragmentations and defragmentation of packets are also responsibilities of Network layer. Even if network protocols are reliable, but packet delivery is not necessarily guaranteed to be reliable. DDoS attack on Network layer basically targets the network devices and resources by flooding them and consuming bandwidth of the resources which significantly reduces overall system performance.

Smurf Attack, ping flood, IP Fragmentation Attacks (Teardrop), IP spoofing and ICMP flood are some of the examples of Network layer attacks. Varrios mitigation techniques are implemented at different network devices to deal with these attacks such as Router Hardening, Geo-IP Filtering, Rate Limiting, Access Control Lists, implement network layer load balancer, Packet Filtering, Anomaly Detection and by using Border-Gateway protocol-based mitigation strategies.

F) Layer 2(Data Link) and Layer 1(Physical) are not typically part of the DDoS Attack classification

Because Layer 2 responsible for assigning MAC address, Framing and Error detection in frames, and Logical link control which basically deal with physical network / Local Area Network (LAN) of network ecosystem. Attacks at this layer such as MAC flooding, ARP spoofing, are local to the network means It comes under category of the Denial of service (DoS) attacks because not scalable, less volumetric, and not distributed in nature.

Layer 1 basically handles signal transmission, data encoding, bit rate control, signal propagation which comes under dealing with hardware devices such as cables, hubs, Network interface cards (NICs), modems. To launch DDoS attack/ DoS attack is practically not ideal as remotely access of this layer is not possible. (Obaid & abeed, 2020 & OSI Model, 2025)

1.1.2. DDoS Mitigations Solutions

1.1.2.1 Collaborative DDoS Mitigation

The idea behind this Collaborative DDoS Mitigation is originated from the nature of DDoS attack as it distributed and collaborative. Majority of attack traffic flow is distributed and targeted victim collaboratively. Collaborative DDoS Mitigation means attack detection, prevention, mitigation and defense performed collaboratively and distributed in nature. In collaborative attack mitigation, all the collaborators mean all the participants who shares common goals of DDoS attack mitigation, collaboratively support each other in terms of attack detection, prevention and mitigation. This is more advanced, critical and outstanding way of attack mitigation as it utilized distributed form of attack mitigation.

By implementing Collaborative mitigation strategies, attack traffic blocked near the source of attack, which is one of the major advantages of collaborative mitigation approach. Devastating effects of attack traffic on other domains, would be reduced significantly as result of blocking attack traffic near attack source. Secondly, repeatedly attack detection, mitigation tasks would be avoided by implementing collaborative DDoS attack mitigation approach, if one domain / network detects attack traffic, by sharing this information, other domains / networks (collaborators) utilized this attack detection information so repetition to discovery the same attack on multiple domains task is avoided. This result in significant resources utilization which incorporate these resources in the productive and necessary tasks of future attack detection and mitigation. Lastly, by signalizing the ongoing attack to other domains, equipped other domains to deal with futuristic attack, and helped them to design attack mitigation strategies beforehand.

In collaborative DDoS mitigation approach, Establishing and maintaining trust between different collaborative parties, networks / domains is key challenge. Additionally, Authenticity and trust on data which shared as a part of mitigation would be difficult to achieve between collaborative domains.

Some collaborative communities that form collaboration and aimed to collaborative DDoS mitigation are the Anti-Phishing Working Group (APWG), the Research and Education Networking (REN) Information Sharing and Analysis Center (REN-ISAC), The Advanced Cyber Defense Centre (ACDC), Internet Engineering Task Force (IETF), and the GÉANT Task Force on Computer Security Incident Response Teams1 (TF-CSIRT).

1.1.2.2 Non-collaborative DDoS Mitigation

Non-collaborative DDoS attack mitigation refers to strategies / methods that individual organization, or third-party Internet Service Providers (ISP) implements independently and without relying on other organization in terms of attack prevention, detection and mitigation. In this approach, organization is fully independent to implement their attack mitigation strategy without intervene of other organization, means it provides more flexibility and control over attack mitigation strategies. As result, Great control over privacy and security of data and network resources are achieved by implementing non-collaborative mitigation strategy. Sometimes while using collaborative migration strategy, latency in terms of attack detection and mitigation, become prevalent, so by implementing non-collaborative attack mitigation one can get rid of this attack mitigation latency issue as attack detection and mitigation performed in the same network cluster.

Contrary, Limitation in terms of available bandwidth and network resources, become prominent factor when relying on non-collaborative DDoS mitigation. Moreover, limited bandwidth and network resources cannot deal with massive and large-scale DDoS attack, for that third-party ISP or collaboration approach would be mandatory requirement. Because to handle massive volume of DDoS attack without any collaboration, it would be more expensive and infeasible in terms of high resources costs and single domain mitigation strategy respectively.

In non-collaborative DDoS mitigation, first, defining normal state of a system by identifying traffic pattern, and traffic behavior is key step in term of DDoS attack identification and detection. This step also involves differentiation between normal traffic and non-human traffic(bots), signature comparison, identification of attributes of attack traffic such as IP addresses, JavaScript footprints, cookies etc. Secondly, Filtering of system traffic based on the criteria decided on previous step. Filtering based on Blacklisted / whitelisted IP addresses, IP Reputation list, Deep packet inspection. In Collaborative / third party system, this work basically performed by dedicated server which filter out the attack traffic from the normal traffic, is basically known as scrubbing servers

/ centers. But in non-collaborative mitigation strategy, it becomes responsibility of the individual organization itself.

Most prominent strategies basically organization which implement non-collaborative approach involves Rate limiting, Access Control List (ACL), robust traffic filtering and monitoring, Anomaly detection systems, in-premises firewalls and Intrusion detection system, and robust verifications system etc.

In real time scenarios, Majority of organizations use Hybrid approach, where collaborative and non-collaborative DDoS attack mitigation strategies combined and utilized for robust DDoS attack mitigation strategy. In Hybrid approach, combination of both approaches such as robust collaboratively attack mitigation's strategies such as resource sharing with individual attack mitigation strategy like Firewall and Intrusion Prevention Systems (IPS) mainly utilized together to get advantages of both approaches. Hybrid approach helps to mitigate large-scale attack without inclusion of additional cost of mitigation infrastructure.

1.2 Blockchain Technology

Blockchain is a distributed ledger technology that securely stored and verifies transactions across multiple distributed nodes without any third-party. Mainly Blockchain technology is the core technology behind Bitcoin and Ethereum cryptocurrencies but use cases of blockchain technology is not limited to it. In blockchain, data integrity and security are maintained using cryptography and digital signature to the stored data. It provides immutable, secured, reliable way to perform transactions in trust-less distributed system.

Purpose behind the Invention of blockchain is to securely transfer tokens in peer-to-peer network. In traditional system, this process involves third-party that manages this transfer process, and act as a central point of trust between sender and receiver of the token. In blockchain Ecosystem, consensus protocols are used to maintain trust between different parties in decentralized manner. (Patel, 2020)

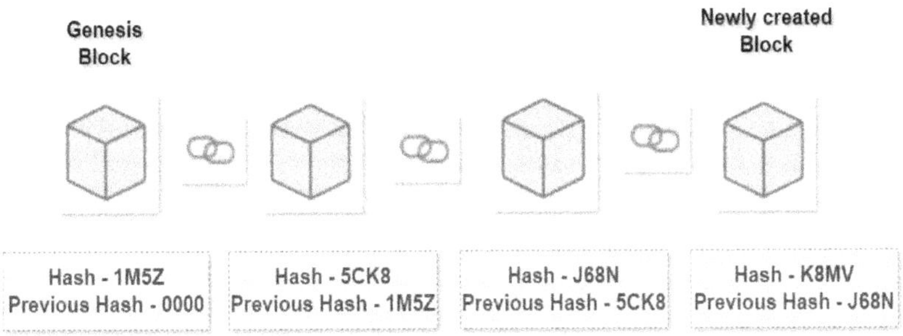

Figure 1.2 Blockchain – Interconnected Blocks

Core concepts of Blockchain Technology:

- **Block** – Smallest unit of blockchain, stores numbers of transactions in it and interconnected with other blocks, to form a chain of blocks. The first block of blockchain is known as Genesis Block. Hash of all the transactions contained in a block along with hash of previous block combinedly computes Block Hash, a pointer of newly created block in Blockchain. The Conceptual block creation and arrangements shown in Figure 1.2.
- **Peer to Peer Network** – Blockchain in general has no fixed protocol and network topology. Blockchain operates on Peer-to-Peer Network, where all

nodes considered at same level, and nodes join and leave blockchain peer-to-peer network at any time without any restrictions. All nodes must maintain a full copy of whole blockchain (Full nodes), which prevents blockchain network from single point of failure.

- **Transactions** – Transactions, Immutable records / piece of data stored in the Blockchain. After miners' validation process, transactions are officially included in the blockchain, by then transaction achieves immutable property and become accessible publicly especially in public blockchain.
- **Mining** – one of the prominent processes in Blockchain network. Mining refers to generation of a new block by solving mathematical computational puzzle. When a new Block get mined at that time pre-decided token of crypto currency get generated because of mining. Mining process consumes more resource and energy (Especially Bitcoin mining process).
- **Consensus** – Consensus basically utilized to establish trust between untrusted parties in Blockchain ecosystem. In simple terms Consensus is a Protocols that ensure all participants agree on the state of the blockchain. It also defines the validity of transaction in a blockchain. Some common examples of consensus mechanisms are Proof of Work (PoW), Proof of Stack (PoS), Proof of Authority (PoA), Proof of Burn (PoB), and Practical Byzantine Fault Tolerance (PBFT).

There are several use cases of Blockchain in real time such as cryptocurrency, supply chain, Healthcare, Digital Finance (DiFi), Non-fungible Tokens (NFT), Security, Finance, Energy sector etc. Mainly Blockchain technology is used decentralized system that established trust in untrusted decentralized environment. And one of the well-known implementations of Blockchain is cryptocurrency.

1.2.1 Types of Blockchain Technology

Blockchain Technology mainly divided into three types:

1.2.1.1 Public Blockchain

A Public blockchain is open, decentralized, public and permissionless blockchain means any one can join and leave blockchain network without any permission and without any intervention of central authority and at any time. This types of blockchain are open and accessible publicly means all the transactions on recorded on the blockchain open to public. Consensus mechanism of public blockchains is designed in such a way that it offers this flexibility in terms of participation and accessibility of the blockchain records. Some of the common characteristics are Open-source, publicly accessible, Anonymous participation, and transparent ledger. Public blockchain are decentralized, highly secured and prevents single points of failure. Contrary, low transaction processing rate, scalability are biggest challenges of public blockchains. Bitcoin, Ethereum, Litecoin are some common examples of it.

1.2.1.2 Private Blockchain

A permissioned and more controlled form of blockchain is a Private blockchain. In Private blockchain, selected group of participants can access, become part of blockchain network and participate in consensus process for transaction processing. Some common characteristics are privacy preserving, more centralized control, Restricted access nature. Mainly enterprises implemented private blockchain for their internal use cases as it provides efficient transaction processing, and privacy over the data. Some Downsides of private blockchain are less secured compared to Public blockchain, more managed and less transparent. Some implementations of private blockchains are Hyperledger Fabric, R3 Corda.

1.2.1.3 Consortium Blockchain

Consortium Blockchain is a type of blockchain where it combines some characteristics of both private and public blockchain to achieve some common goals. Consortium Blockchain is basically governed by selected group of entities that known as consortium group, not owned by any private enterprise or fully public (means partially decentralized). It is more balanced approach between decentralization and control. Basically, consortium blockchain is formed to fulfill some common goals of society such as banking consortium, energy consortium. These consortium groups are responsible for to design rules for accessibility of blockchain, consensus mechanism, governance and control. Some common characteristics of this blockchain are controlled by consortium group, faster than public blockchain, high throughput and scalability. Infrastructure complexity and less adoption rate compared to public blockchains are some challenges of it. Some common examples include Dragonchain, Energy web chain, We.trade etc. (Blockchain, 2025)

1.3 Leverage Blockchain Technology in DDoS attacks Mitigation

DDoS attacks become more devastating and adverse these days by targeting availability of the existing system in this internet ecosystem. System Availability is a crucial when many existing system trades of between availability and eventual consistency. Majority of systems choose system availability over eventual consistency as more and more digitization of existing systems. Disruption in system availability leads to adverse effect on overall system as well as suffers reputation of system.

To deal with this adverse and distributed nature of attack, it would be advisable to design solution which also occupy the same as a solution. Blockchain technology would be the perfect to design solution to deal with DDoS attack as blockchain has properties such as distributed, transparent, decentralized, secured and immutable etc. Because of distributed nature of blockchain technology, it is increasingly being explored as a solution to mitigate Distributed Denial-of-Service (DDoS) attacks.

Blockchain Technology used as a solution to mitigate DDoS attack in various ways: Firstly, Decentralized Infrastructure: By using the blockchain technology, existing infrastructure of the system get distributed across the various distributed nodes of blockchain, which prevents system from single point of failure. And provides many advantages like distribute load across servers, and faster response rate. Secondly, Blockchain used to serve Domain Name Server (DNS) in decentralized manner, which helps DNS servers from single point of failure and provides immutability of records in DNS servers for backtracking and verification. ENS (Ethereum Name Service) is one of the most notable examples of blockchain based DNS.

Blockchain based Content Delivery Networks (CDN) is one of the wide use cases where blockchain is utilized for the DDoS mitigation. CDN are basically used serving static content sometimes also help to serve live streaming data. Blockchain based CDN helps to distributes load across multiple servers and prevents single server failure. Lastly, Smart contracts used for traffic filtering: smart contract is a self-executing program stored on blockchain, basically an agreement which auto-executes when predefined conditions are met. Smart contracts are used to very traffic logs, store traffic related data, analysis of traffic data etc.

1.4 Organization of Thesis

This thesis is planned in such a way that it is divided into five chapters. First chapter presented brief introduction of DDoS attack and its mitigation strategies along with Blockchain Technology. As well as this chapter also focused on Utilization of Blockchain technology for DDoS attack Mitigation and some core objectives, contribution and limitation of this research work.

In Chapter two, a brief literature review of research work carried out in field of Blockchain Technology and Cyber Security especially in DDoS attack. The research studies of utilization of blockchain for DDoS mitigation is also briefly covered in this chapter.

Chapter three discusses about Research design and overall research methodology of the proposed solution. Additionally, the proposed Collaborative DDoS mitigation approach, Blockchain selection, Blockchain based infrastructure selection and data generation are also presented in this Chapter.

In Chapter four we presented the Proposed System Architecture. Then after, the framework of the proposed solution which divided into Collaborative mitigation scheme and Intra-network scheme are briefly defined in this Chapter.

The Chapter five demonstrated the implementation of the proposed solution. In this chapter, we also defined implementation of the proposed solution over three different environments – such as controlled environment, Distributed network and real network. Additionally, Simulation of Volumetric DDoS attacks on Distributed Network are presented.

The Last Chapter six dedicated for result and discussion of the proposed solution. the experimental results of the experiments performed over three different environments are defined briefly. Then we presented performance evaluation of the proposed solution. and finally, this thesis ends with conclusion and future direction of the proposed research.

CHAPTER 2: RESEARCH BACKGROUND AND LITERATURE REVIEW

2.1. Utilization of Blockchain Technology in Mitigation of various Cyber Attacks and Networks Threats

In Cyber security Ecosystem, Usage of Blockchain Technology to mitigate various adverse cyber-attacks and threads are emerging and full of new opportunities. As Blockchain has built in characteristics such as immutability, decentralization and security provide great potential to build a new solution on top of existing blockchain or leveraging blockchain for cyber threat mitigation. Most prominent use cases of Blockchain Technology in Cyber security ecosystems are defined in this section.

Authors	**Years**	**Key Area covered**	**Utilization of Blockchain**
(Nasir et al., 2023)	2023	Intrusion Detection System (IDS), device-level botnet detection, Internet of Things (IoT)	Attack signature sharing, trust values
(Sagirlar et al., 2018)	2018	Botnet detection mechanism, IoT	Byzantine Fault Tolerant (BFT) blockchain used as a state transition machine
(Lu et al., 2018)	2018	Vehicular ad-hoc networks, Trust management, Reputation System	A blockchain-based anonymous reputation system (BARS), Reputation system
(Agarkar et al., 2024)	2024	Identity management, Access Control, public key cryptography	Ethereum based blockchain to store identity data
(Salem & Daraghmi, 2021)	2021	Blockchain, privacy, Compliance	Blockchain used for GDPR compliances

(Conti et al., 2022)	2022	CDN, data privacy, security	Private blockchain based on Proof of Authority
(Shah et al., 2023)	2023	DNS, privacy, security, DNS threats, DDoS attack	DNS based records stored in blockchain, Consortium blockchain
(Careja & Tapus, 2023)	2023	Digital Identity, public key, private key, Elliptic Curve, privacy	Ethereum blockchain used to store data and transactions
(Chatziamanetoglou & Rantos, 2023)	2023	Cyber threat intelligence (CTI), Reputation and trust based mechanism	CTI data sharing using blockchain, proof-of-quality (PoQ) consensus mechanism
(Austin & Di Troia, 2023)	2023	Logging, Tamper-resistance, Proof of Work(PoW)	Proof of work based blockchain used to store system logs data
(Rai et al., 2024)	2024	Data privacy, Security, IoT, Energy sector	Proof of Work (PoW) and Proof of Stake (PoS) consensus mechanism

[Table 2.1: Literature Review – Utilization of Blockchain for Cyber-attacks and Network Threats Mitigation]

(Nasir et al., 2023) This paper presents a collaborative approach through which detection of Botnet for IoT by implementing IDS on the IoT device level, hence increase in overall device level security. Combination of Signature based detection system with trusted signature updates are used as an input for the IDS. And this signature-based IDS approach is evaluated through various IoT datasets such as ISOT, IoT23, BotIoT. In this paper, BTC_SIGBDS (Blockchain-powered, Trustworthy, Collaborative, Signature based Botnet Detection System) was also introduced which group together this signature-based IDS with reputation system and secured blockchain technology. Author utilized blockchain for secure information sharing, trust management between different entries but implementation of the blockchain related details is not included the paper. Additionally, this signature based IoT botnet detection work implemented on which specific blockchain is not explicitly mentioned, but the conceptualization of paper leverages any private or permissioned blockchain for collaboration purpose. For the detection of device level botnet through signature-based IDE Snort and Suricata were implemented. This framework detects TCP based DoS / DDoS attack, with high accuracy by implementing device level signature-based approach in IoT Ecosystem.

(Sagirlar et al., 2018) AutoBotCatcher (proposed approach of this paper) detects the Botnets by observing communication patterns of different bots by observing traffic flows and identifies the bot communities. In this paper, Author proposed A permissioned byzantine Fault Tolerance (BFT) blockchain as a state transition machine that facilitates open and transparent collaboration between predefined parties in untrusted environment. For Collaborative Botnet detection, IoT devices traffic flows metadata are recorded as a blockchain transaction and sharing among predefined collaborators. For botnet community detection, Louvain method implemented on evolving mutual-contacts graphs for botnet clusters. For result analysis, performance matrix or any empirical data is not provided. This paper mainly presents the architectural design and integration of blockchain for botnet detection. It is stated that this AutoBotCatcher is scalable, efficient and secure solution to detect botnet among IoT gateways by leveraging blockchain technology.

(Lu et al., 2018) The proposed System, BARS leverages blockchain for maintaining privacy of vehicles in vehicle as-hoc networks (VANETS), also prevents linkability of public key with real identity of vehicle and tracking attack prevention. Two blockchains are used to transparency in certificate issue and revocation process. Authors used three different blockchains for different purposes: CerBC (Certificates Blockchain) that records certificate insurance, RevBC (Revocations Blockchain) for certificate revocation and MesBC (Messages Blockchain): which stores all the broadcasted messages for persistent evidence for reputation updates. Direct interactions and indirect opinions of the vehicle's details aggregated on-chain, used to calculates reputation score of the vehicle. Some limitations of BARS scheme noticed during its implementation such as storage limitation, cryptographic overhead and security validation. But overall, BARS scheme presents an efficient privacy preserving and decentralized mechanism in vehicle ad-hoc networks (VANETS) by implementing blockchains along with reputation and trust management system.

(Agarkar et al., 2024) In this paper, author defined a blockchain-aware decentralized identity management and access control (BADIMAC) model that helps users to take charge of their digital identity in this internet ecosystem by using blockchain based approach. Additionally, users can verify their digital identity without interference of centralized authority or third party across various enterprises. BADIMAC model relies on decentralized consensus-based design to validate digital identity of user in efficient and secured way. Private Ethereum based blockchain utilized for mange central point of trust and Ethereum smart contracts for decentralized identity management and access control in untrusted environment. For different roles in identity management process such as Identity owner, Identity verifier, service providers, identity provider, Ethereum's account-based model utilized for storing various identity providers information and logging purpose over blockchain. The BADIMAC model implemented on Ethereum TestNet and access control mechanism are designed as on-chain smart contracts for evaluating user claims and granting-relocating permissions. This model tries to provide Single Sign On and JSON Web Token (JWT) functionality through Ethereum based blockchain based infrastructure is efficient and scalable solution. Contrary, Ethereum gas fees for smart contract and single point of failure as deployment of solution on private, permissioned blockchain become considerable factors while leveraging this model as a solution.

Salem & Daraghmi, 2021 This systematic review paper provides in depth exploration of Blockchain technology in GDPR compliance. Blockchain technology has inbuilt features such as cryptographical secured, distributed, immutable, transparent enables it as a solution for personal data security standards of GDPR. In this paper, author discussed briefly on blockchain technology and GDPR components, principles and GDPR rights. Then authors tried to map blockchain characteristics to various GDPR articles. By systematized all this information, author proposed four key suggestions on improving compliancy of blockchain with GDPR standards such as Encryption, Permissioned blockchain, Hash and Central Server for off-chain storage and Zero-knowledge proof. Smart contracts also play prominent role in consent and policy enforcement in GDPR domain. Author also depicted various studies and research in this field to provide more relevant context in leverage of blockchain for GDPR compliance.

Conti et al., 2022 In this paper, author proposed a secured CDN by leveraging proof of Authority based private blockchains. This solution leveraged blockchain so that trust management, single point of failure and tempering of data related issues resolved by inherent characteristics of the blockchain. In this proposed system, two private blockchains based on Proof of Authority (PoA) utilized for the design of a secured CDN. The first blockchain called Content blockchain served as a CDN network, mainly utilized for serving the content over all the edge servers (blockchain nodes). End users are restricted to access to this blockchain. The second blockchain named Check Blockchain's main purpose is to check received object integrity by using inbuilt hash mechanism of blockchain, which enables offline or intermittent verification. Smart contracts are used for content registration and hash updates of on-chain transaction and logging purpose. Prototype of this solution is deployed on Ethereum blockchain and solidity based Ethereum blockchain. Clients are responsible to maintain state of blockchain so that eliminates blockchain storage and cost problem. Additionally, the experimental analysis shows that proposed solution is efficient and scalable to serve CDN network.

Shah et al., 2023 Authors presented Blockchain enabled Domain Name System (DNS) that mainly aimed to enhance security DNS systems along with that mitigate various attacks on the DNS system such as DDoS attacks, security breaches of DNS. As DNS security is crucial to achieve, and if any threats and security breaches in DNS affects all the three aspects of the system - confidentiality, integrity, and availability, hence DNS security is a key concern. In this paper, author's focused on designing blockchain enabled DNS system to mitigate DDoS attacks on DNS system as DDoS attacks have left adverse effects on all the three aspects of DNS system. The proposed architecture worked on all the levels of DNS system from registrar (top-level domain) to client. Here author used decentralized nature of blockchain to design a blockchain based solution for DNS that defense the DDoS attacks efficiently, and without any central point of failure. In this proposed solution, a private permissioned Ethereum based blockchain utilized for smart contracts deployments and DNS records, zone files storage. Various registration and revocation smart contracts used for creating / updating new DNS records. As DNS records stored on-chain, Recursive resolvers computes the hash of DNS records and verifies with the on-chain DNS records which would be beneficial in tempering detection of the DNS records. This proposed solution not only mitigates DDoS attacks but also helpful for various DNS attacks such as Cache Poisoning and Spoofing & Hijacking

Mitigation. By evaluating the performance matrix, proposed blockchain based solution is scalable, efficient and resilient against DDoS attacks on DNS system.

Careja & Tapus, 2023 This paper demonstrates a self-sovereign digital identity model ensures privacy, validity and integrity of user data by utilizing blockchain technology and cryptography. For Integrity and security of the user data, cryptographic signatured used, which issued by the trusted authorities, and these signature data further recorded on the blockchain. Elliptic Curve Digital Signature Algorithm (ECDSA) used for signing digital identity of users. This proposed solution deployed on private Ethereum blockchain and smart contracts to manage identity issuance, revocation, and access checks. The trusted authorities record user signatures and attributes on Ethereum blockchain. The verifiers recompute the hash and reverifies this against the blockchain transactions which prerecorded by the trusted authorities. The experimental result of this model shows that latency and throughput is averaged under 1 second and as it is deployed on private blockchain, so cost is also comparatively low. By using this model, multi-participant decision support systems enhance its decision-making capability as inherent secured and immutable nature of blockchain.

Chatziamanetoglou & Rantos, 2023 In this paper, authors proposed a Cyber Threat intelligence (CTI) framework that collects, stores and disseminates this data by leveraging blockchain technology to utilize inherent characteristic of it and make this CTI sharing process more transparent and trustworthy. Additionally, a reputation system is also implemented to choose validator peers that further rates this CTI feeds. Validator selection process involves proof-of-Quality consensus mechanism which ensures fairness of the process and exclusion of low-quality peers from the validation process. and the on-chain CTI data is further considered to evaluate reputation of CTI sources. CTI data collected through multiple sources such as by using sensors and commercial feeds and ingested into the system, then Reputation system rated the CTI data (In this stage validator validated the CTI data by reaching consensus and then these data published on-chain). The private permissioned blockchain employed for restricting participation of known CTI sources for the purpose of maintain performance and access control of the system. In this paper, author provides only theoretical Model simulation using probabilistic approach. By evaluating this simulation results, the Proof of Quality fairness is recorded as low quality validators eliminated from the system, and feed fairness is comparatively high when compare with stack-based scheme. Along with that, tempering with on-chain CTI records also detected which highlights temper resistant nature of solution thanks to inherit blockchain nature. Overall, proposed solution is efficient, scalable and termer-proof CTI sharing solution in cyber threat sharing ecosystem.

Austin & Di Troia, 2023 Authors represents a temper resistant logging framework which leveraged proof-of-work consensus based blockchain for the purpose of immutability of logs stored on the blockchain. Additionally, various techniques used for compromising the logs data are discussed and statistical result of this evasion techniques are presented in this paper. To design this blockchain based temper resistant logging framework, Authors used SpartanGold blockchain, an experimental blockchain especially designed for educational purpose, and enhance the functionality of this blockchain by adding capability like smart contracts. All logs are grouped together and stored in a single node Proof of Work (PoW) blockchain by using PoW based mining (by solving cryptographic puzzle). Attackers (Entity who attack for purpose of tempering Log data) need to rewrite or recompute the PoW based puzzle of all the blocks of blockchain even if attackers took complete control of single block, which would be more computationally expensive. And which makes logs data secured and immutable in under attack situation, which is the unique and significant feature of this framework. Moreover, this framework runs on single private node so no additional requirements or dependency to connect with public blockchain. This framework utilized Proof of Work consensus to store log data on blockchain which provides immutability of data without any need of decentralized blockchain implementation, which makes model more effective along with that statistical anomaly detection system implemented in this model, enhances the detection capability of this framework.

Rai et al., 2024 This paper represents the comprehensive study of integration of Blockchain technology and IoT in nuclear energy Applications. This study also discusses opportunities, challenges, various roles, and dimensions of this integration on nuclear energy applications. From this comprehensive study, authors identified the security and privacy challenges as a research gap and proposed a secure data management framework that fulfills these research gaps. In this paper, A flowchart-based study of utilization of blockchain in energy domain also presents the security and privacy challenges. In this paper, authors were not explicitly mentioned utilization of which specific blockchain to implement proposed framework but by observing the research work it might be assume that private/permissioned blockchain runs by trusted energy organization. In this work, blockchain was utilized to store hashed of sensor registration data, alerts acknowledgements as immutability and security features of blockchain. Authors stated that this research in blockchain and IoT domain significantly improves security and privacy of nuclear energy applications however with some optimization and validation challenges.

2.2. Blockchain Technology Towards Mitigation of Distributed Denial of Service Attacks

In this section, by narrow down the scope of this literature review, we discussed how blockchain Technology utilized to mitigate one of the adverse cyber-attacks by reviewing various research papers of this domain. Prominent research works in Blockchain and DDoS mitigation domain, we broadly categorized it into four sections – based on utilization of Blockchain Technology as solution to mitigate DDoS attacks.

2.2.1. Blockchain Technology used as a Collaborative Medium

In this first category, Blockchain technology served as a collaborative medium in DDoS attack mitigation. Basically, Blockchain serves in three different ways when leverage it as a collaborative Medium:

- Becomes medium to share attack information to other collaborators
- Acts as a transparent medium for attack prevention, detection and defense
- Provides a transparency between collaborators in untrusted environment

Authors	Years	Key Area covered	Utilization of Blockchain
17. (Patel & Patel, 2023)	2023	Blockchain, Collaborative DDoS mitigation	Attack signature sharing, Smart Contracts
18. (Patel & Patel, 2024)	2024	Collaborative approach, DDoS mitigation, attack detection	Blockchain used for attack information sharing,

19. (Abou El Houda et al., 2019)	2019	Collaboration, Entropy, Computer Crime	Ethereum based blockchain used for sharing attack data
20. (Rodrigues et al., 2020)	2020	Blockchain, Software defined Networking (SDN), Security management	Blockchain used for forming collaboration between peers
21. (Jiang et al., 2022)	2022	Attack detection and mitigation, SDN domain	By using blockchain and smart contracts
22. (A et al., 2024)	2024	Blockchain, DDoS mitigation, Machine learning	Ethereum blockchain used to maintain list of blacklisted IPs

[Table 2.2: Literature Review – Utilization of Blockchain as Collaborative Medium]

Existing Solutions	Category (Prevention, Defense, Mitigation)	Implemented Blockchain	How the Collaborative Approach implemented	Additional Security requirements	Domain Intra/Inter	Incentive Scheme
(Hameed and Khan 2019)	Attack Detection, Mitigation	No	- Controller-to-controller protocol for communication - Used Software-Defined Networking	- Certificate authority(POX-Controller generated	Both	No
(Rodrigues et al, 2020)	Defense and Mitigation in Autonomous System	Yes(Ethereum)	- Smart contracts deployed on Ethereum and permissioned Proof-of-Authority(PoA) Ethereum Blockchain - By signaling attacks and incentive mechanism	- Encryption and decryption - Transport layer security	Both	Yes
(Moriarty 2012)	- Not provided - However, existing detection, tracing, source identification, and mitigation mechanisms were integrated.	No	- To facilitate sharing incident-handling data - Build own inter-domain communication system through XML. - By Consortiums and Public Key Infrastructures	- XML digital signature and Encryption - Public key infrastructure	Both	No
Boucadair et al., 2022	- Collaborative Internet standard for attack detection, mitigation - Works at the Autonomous System(ISP) Level	No	- For communication, HTTP is used - Through Client-server Architecture	Https with TLS(for protocol security)	Both	No
(Rashidi and Fung 2016)	- Provided Defense mechanism	No	- Using Network Function Virtualization(NVF) through Virtual ISP	Using a Virtual ISP(Communication Component)	Inter	No
(Abou El Houda et al. 2019)	Attack detection and mitigation are provided	Yes(Ethereum)	- Using Ethereum smart contracts to share attack information	Smart contract security	Both	No
(Bremler-barr and Sabag 2022)	Provided Detection, Mitigation, and attack signaling	No	- By using DDoS Open Threat Signaling(DOTS) protocol	Https with TLS(for protocol security)	Inter	Yes
(Jiang et al. 2022)	Provided Detection and Mitigation in the SDN domain	Yes	- By using Blockchain and Smart Contracts	Secure Middle Plane consists of threat collecting and smart contract APIs.	Both	No

[Table 2.3: Existing DDoS Mitigation Solution – Comparative Analysis]

Note: - Reproduced from Volumetric Distributed Denial of Service Attacks Mitigation using Polygon Blockchain – A Collaborative Approach, by Darshi Patel and Dhiren Patel, 2024, Science and Technology Journal (STJ) , Vol 12, issue 1, pg. 155-164.

Patel & Patel, 2023 In this paper, authors proposed a blockchain based collaborative solution to mitigate volume-based DDoS attacks. This collaborative framework named PolyDDoSchain, utilized blockchain technology to build transparent and secured collaboration between multiple networks(collaborators) in untrusted environment. Volumetric DDoS attack detection and mitigation performed collaboratively by leveraging Polygon smart contracts and Polygon blockchain, a layer 2 solution of Ethereum blockchain. This PolyDDoSchain framework consists of Intra-domain and Inter-domain mitigation of volumetric DDoS attacks. In Intra-domain mitigation architecture, a collaborator's network inbound and outbound traffic from the internet directly faced by Snort, an Intrusion Detection System (IDS) then filtered traffic reached to the network. In this process, Snort identified any blacklisted IP addresses are shared on Polygon blockchain smart contracts and this blacklisted IP address file stored in IPFS, A decentralized File storage system. Polygon blockchain and smart contracts formed a collaboration between different networks(collaborators) transparent and efficient in Inter-domain DDoS mitigation architecture. From implementation perspective, Polygon's TestNet, Mumbai Test Network used to deploy the Polygon smart contracts written in Solidity (A language to write smart contract). And simulation results are presented and discussed in this paper. By implementing this PolyDDoSchain repeated attack detection and mitigation tasks are avoided as solution built on collaborative mechanism. As well as, Because of blockchain based solution, single point of failure of collaborator(network) is also avoided, and inbuilt characteristics of blockchain technology such as immutability, security and transparency provided extra layer of data Secuity to the on-chain data. By evaluating its experimental results, It is stated that proposed framework is secured, easy to deploy and cost-effective solution in Collaborative DDoS mitigation domain .

Patel & Patel, 2024 This paper presents a collaborative solution to mitigate volumetric DDoS attacks by using Blockchain Technology. This proposed ColPolyDDoSMitigation application leverages Polygon Blockchain, a permission-less blockchain to share attack signatures to other collaborators networks. This proposed framework also build transparent collaboration between peers using Polygon blockchain. By Utilizing ColPolyDDoSMitigation Decentralized Application (DApp), collaborators(networks) register itself on the Polygon blockchain. This DApp deployed on the Polygon's official TestNet, Mumbai TestNet. This DApps also provides facility to share attack signatures between all the peers(collaborators). These Smart contracts implementations details, and execution details are also provided in this paper. This proposed solution implemented on various system and different statistics and comparisons are briefly discussed. By evaluating this matrix, it clearly indicates that Proposed solution is cost effective as smart contract deployment cost is comparatively very less and performance is significantly improved and Time to deploy smart contract is decreased as compared to other collaborative solutions.

Abou El Houda et al., 2019 This paper represents a Cochain-SC framework that mitigate DDoS attacks collaboratively by leveraging Blockchain technology and SDN. In this paper, authors presented two-tiered approach to mitigate DDoS attacks where in Intra-domain attack detection in context of SDN various method such as Intra Entropy-based scheme(I-ES), Intra Bayes-based scheme(I-BS) and Intra-domain Mitigation(I-DM) were implemented. These detection methods used machine learning based algorithms for efficiently detect attack signature in context to SDN in Autonomous Systems(AS) (collaborator network), a broad ISP level Networks. Whereas a blockchain based framework, which built using Ethereum Blockchain and smart contracts implemented for attack information sharing among various participant networks (AS) in Inter-domain scheme. By combining both the domain, makes this Cochain-SC framework as a complete solution to detect and mitigate any ongoing attack near the source of attack means detected traffic blocked in source Autonomous System reduce the overhead of traffic flow and detection in other intermediate and destination domains. Proposed framework deployed on Ethereum TestNet name Ropsten test network, and attack simulation details are also provided in the paper. By studying these statistics, this proposed solution is efficient cost-effective, secured and flexible and achieved high attack detection accuracy in context to SDN and efficiently block attack near the source Autonomous System by utilizing Ethereum blockchain based collaborative solution.

Rodrigues et al., 2020 In this Paper, author a blockchain based framework named BloSS, one of the collaborative DDoS attacks signaling framework in cyber security ecosystem. BloSS introduced a secured, distributed framework that leveraged blockchain technology for cooperative DDoS attacks signaling among various AS. Authors also presented an incentive mechanism which built on smart contracts for reduce free riding of collaborators in distributed system and provide more authenticity to the on-chain data. This cooperative framework has capability of detection and mitigation and blocked the attack traffic near source of attacks. Each SDN based controlled employed Entropy-Based & Bayesian technique for attack detection and identification in near real time. And these attack signatures were shared through smart contracts to other AS systems (Collaborators). Smart contract-based reputation system constantly updated the reputation scores of collaborators based on the attack signatures. The BloSS framework is deployed on Ethereum' official TestNet name Ropsten, and smart contract and its deployment information provided in the paper. The prototype of this BloSS solution is implemented globally through cloud service providers. From evaluating the system statistics proposed system has high attack detection rate means 95% of true positive rate and only 3% of false positive in SDN based intra-domain. Contrary, as every attack signature stored in smart contracts, which cause performance overhead and less optimized in terms of cost. overall, Bloss framework is blockchain based scalable, efficient and distributed framework in collaborative attack mitigation space.

Jiang et al., 2022 Motivation behind this Paper is that existing DDoS mitigation solution designed for single SDN controller could not provide efficient mitigation for multiple SDN controllers as absence of collaboration mechanism between these multiple SDN controllers. So, authors came up with a blockchain based collaborative solution especially designed to integrate multiple SDN based controller efficiently in distributed and secured manner, and presented collaborative solution named BSD-Guard. In this proposed framework, a blockchain based middle plane acted employed between control plane and data plane, acted as a medium that collects flow statistics, SDN rule controller and reported attack data to the blockchain. Here, authors utilized a private, permissioned blockchain to deploy smart contracts, that served as a medium for collaboration and attack information sharing between multiple SDN based controllers.

The simulation of this blockchain is deployed on Ropten TestNet of Ethereum on both public and private blockchain. For attack detection on SND domain, employed three detection techniques such as entropy, Bayesian, flow-rule enforcement on SDN controller level and smart contracts served as collaboration and logging purposes. This BDS-Guard acheived high detection accuracy with only 3% false positive rate, highly scalable as deployed over blockchain. But still, high latency, network overhead and high cost are some downsides of this model because of Ethereum based blockchain implementation and smart contracts executions.

A et al., 2024 In this paper, Authors represents a novel system where a classification-based machine learning technique used for DDoS attack detection in intra-domain and blockchain technology for sharing blacklisted IP addresses by utilizing capability of SDN in inter-domain mitigation. This proposed framework used Canadian Institute of Cyber Security's CICDDoS2019 dataset (for distinguish legitimate packets from malicious packets) to train and test the classification-based machine learning technique. Ethereum based blockchain is used to share attack data (malicious IP addresses) identified by the Artificial Neural Network (ANN) based machine learning model. SDN controllers were employed to get on-chain blacklisted IP address data and installed flow-drop rules in other controllers to effectively block illegitimate attack traffic. This proposed framework is deployed on private Ethereum blockchain (Ganache simulated private blockchain used for smart contracts evocations and SDN based node collaborations. This blockchain based architectures provides immutability and security to the on-chained stored attack information and become a collaborative medium in untrusted environment. For feature extraction for model Chi-Square Test is used. The Mininet simulator is used to simulate SDN based domains and attack ecosystem. By carefully evaluating research statistics, it is stated that the ANN achieved 72.49% of accuracy in DDoS attacks detection in Mininet. Overall, this proposed framework achieved high detection accuracy by efficiently choosing right machine learning technique and efficient attack mitigation in collaborative space by empowering Blockchain technology.

2.2.2. Blockchain based CDN for DDoS attack Mitigation

The main role of Content Delivery Network (CDN) is to deliver media and streaming data to end user by efficiently transferring the content near to end user location (Edge servers) for better performance and enhance user experience. This CDN technology has great potential when employ it for DDoS attack mitigation. Especially CDN used for efficiently route the traffic and used to share network resources to other networks while under-attack situation. This systematic review defines how Blockchain based CDN empowered DDoS attack detection and mitigation in cyber security ecosystem.

Authors	Years	Key Area covered	Utilization of Blockchain
(Kim et al., 2018)	2018	DDoS Mitigation, private blockchain, CDN	Private blockchain, Proof-of-Concept based protocol
(Gladius Network, 2017)	2017	DDoS protection, CDN, Blockchain	Token based, blockchain used to build collaboration
(Conti et al., 2022)	2022	Blockchain, CDN, Static CDN	Proof of concept based blockchain
(Yousafzai et al., 2021)	2021	Peer to peer, CDN	Blockchain based cryptocurrency, smart contract

[Table 2.4: Literature Review – Blockchain based CDN for DDoS attacks Mitigation]

Kim et al., 2018 In this paper, authors shed light on the problem of transparency, security and coordination between different CDN utilized especially for DDoS attacks mitigation because of centralized nature of CDN. And to solve this problem, authors utilized a private blockchain that stores CDN schema information on-chain for efficiently provide transparency, security and reliability to different CDN in unreliable environment. Authors defines a distributed CDN framework by leveraging permissioned private blockchain to pool spare bandwidth across authorized nodes, resulting improve mitigation capability of single CDN and prevents single point of failure. A Byzantine Fault Tolerance (BFT) algorithm in private permissioned blockchain to prevent public blockchain problems such as validity of Tokens and unpredictable block conformation timing. In each block, contract data of authenticated bandwidth such as IP ranges, provider metadata, and Merkle-root proofs were stored to provide authenticity, security, auditability and integrity of these log data. In this proposed blockchain framework, Permissioned Node (Block Generator), Bandwidth Provider were participated, where Bandwidth providers act as a public blockchain or existing CDN. And role of these providers node was to distribute bandwidth and set of permissions to borrower nodes. Only authorized nodes can perform any operations in the proposed system, and both nodes first exchange their public keys to each other for further communication and to establish contract for attack mitigation. Authors simulated a tradition CDN and a blockchain based distributed CDN and adjusting various parameters. By considering all the factors, authors stated that a blockchain based schema is more distributed, so it becomes difficult for attackers to identify and attack the critical cache node of the CDN. This proposed solution is robust, secured and scalable solution in CDN space.

Gladius Network LLC, 2017 This proposed solution named Gladius solution, is a distributed CDN based solution that utilized CDN based blockchain mainly for through resource sharing in transparent, distributed and secured way. Gladius solution aimed to provide DDoS attacks protection and low cost CDN services in some extents by utilizing unused network resources and storage of the CDN networks in decentralized manner by leveraging blockchain. For this Gladius Network launched that fixed numbers of GLA tokens based on Ethereum's ERC-20, to incentivize the collaborators(operator) nodes, and (deployed smart contracts for) rewards distributions for among network collaborators. This GLA tokens are given to the networks that facilitated their unused bandwidth for decentralized CDN. This Gladius solution can neutralize the DDoS traffic through geographical distributed CDN and caching servers. In decentralized CDN architecture of Gladius solution, two types of nodes involved: Peer Nodes, that advertise their available bandwidth and storage, and Protection Nodes are the nodes who requests DDoS protection services or CDN services in the Gladius distributed network. And these Gladius solution combines all the Peers Nodes bandwidth in proxy pool and facilitates these bandwidths to Protection Nodes upon request. All these interactions data are recorded on-chains, which provides transparency, security and integrity to the contracts data. In this paper, implementation details are not given. By Gladius solution claimed that this proposed model is secured, efficient and incentive proof mechanism to prevent and mitigate DDoS attack by leveraging a blockchain based decentralized CDN.

Conti et al., 2022 In this paper, authors represent a blockchain based CDN that secured CDN data and prevent the adverse problem of single point of failure of CDN nodes without relying on central authority. In this solution, this proposed framework mainly focused on static CDN content such as images, video not live or streaming content, by employing a proof-of-concept mechanism through private Ethereum based blockchain. This proposed solution implemented two Ethereum based blockchains, Content blockchain that serves as a static content storage of CDN network. And Check blockchain logs all the transactional hashes of the Content blockchain. In this Content blockchain, actual edge servers act as a node in this blockchain and authorized content creators directly upload the static content over this blockchain nodes. So that central admin, who manages content related information and issues directly eliminated from the proposed system. And from client side, client verifies the origin and authenticity content by verifies the hash of content recorded on the Check blockchain. Client can report the server(node) that provided tempered static content in the system and based on these reporting data and some other factors, servers(nodes) reputation scores calculated. The prototype implementation of proposed system on Ethereum TestNet are given in this paper. By evaluating various statistics, it is defined that proposed solution achieves high performance as used SHA3-256 hash to calculates hash of static content, and storage efficient as it used Merkle Trees for content hashes and static content's storage.

Yousafzai et al., 2021 This paper tried to solve the problem of Peer-to-Peer CDN such as peer churning and free riding as absence of any incentive mechanism for participating in Peer-to-Peer network by introducing a cryptographic based crowdsourced Peer to Peer CDN scheme. In this Paper authors represent a cryptocurrency incentivized crowdsourced P2P CDN (CROWD-CDN) for resolving these two problems of P2P CDN systems. This proposed model named CROWD-CDN incentivizes all its peer contributors(collaborators) networks based upon its contribution to the overall CDN content distribution capacity by using its blockchain and smart contract backed cryptocurrency scheme. This proposed scheme used container-enabled peer nodes virtualization for Peer's contribution monitoring and securely store CDN's content in isolated container located at peer's network. The prominent contribution of these CROWD-CDN is a cryptocurrency-based Peer to Peer CDN scheme implemented by utilizing blockchain and smart contract that provides scalable and secure content delivery to end user along with security and privacy of Peer's devices are also considered while designing this proposed scheme. Additionally, this scheme also prevents unauthorized access of service providers (content creator's) content in the seed supplying peers. Authors simulated this CROWD-CDN scheme by utilizing blockchain and smart contract based blockchain for incentives the contributors in Peer-to-Peer distributed CDN ecosystem. In this paper, authors tried to provide various variants of these proposed CROWD-CDN scheme by leveraging testbed setup and evaluated this cryptography-based incentive mechanism.

2.2.3. Blockchain based DNS for DDoS attack Mitigation

Domain Name Server (DNS) is the hierarchical, distributed mapping service which translates human-readable domains name into IP addresses, and serves this naming services to computers, web-services and other resources on internet Ecosystem. In DNS system, many servers such as Recursive Resolver, root servers, Authoritative Name Servers, and TLD Servers are involved in Name Resolution Process and handles various DNS record types. The DNS system plays prominent role in internet ecosystem, so some factors are significantly important in DNS system implementation such as decentralized and scalable system as it prevents whole system from single point of failure, performance for that caching system servers fast and efficient delivery and able to handle various types of records and security of DNS ecosystem as growing attacks on DNS systems. By evaluating these system design requirements, Blockchain technology would become perfect choice to design secure, scalable, efficient and distributed DNS system as blockchain has many inbuilt features play a prominent role in DNS system design. This sub-section represents various prominent research work where innovative utilization of blockchain technology to resolve various design challenges of DNS Ecosystems.

Authors	Years	Key Area covered	Utilization of Blockchain
(Shah et al., 2023)	2023	DNS, privacy, security, DNS threats, DDoS attack	DNS based records stored in blockchain, Consortium blockchain
(Ali et al., 2016)	2016	Blockchain, DNS, storage, PKI	Blockchain based PKI, public proof of work blockchain
(Kalodner et al., 2015)	2015	DNS, cryptocurrency, Blockchain, DNS based threads	Blockchain used to store DNS based records
(Li et al., 2021)	2021	DNS, Cache Poisoning Attack, DDoS Attack.	a Proof-of-Stake (PoS) consensus protocol, an index of domains
(Xia et al., 2021)	2021	DNS, blockchain, DNS threats	Ethereum based blockchain for DNS

[Table 2.5: Literature Review – Blockchain based DNS for DDoS attacks Mitigation]

Shah et al., 2023 For full review of this paper, defined in Section 2.1, Review Paper number – 12. In this paper, Authors focus on enhancing security of DNS system and prevents DNS systems from various vulnerabilities and attacks by implementing blockchain based DNS scheme. In this paper, author, presented a blockchain based DNS system that enhanced overall DNS system security and countermeasures to DDoS attacks. Blockchain served as a distributed DNS system as a result risk of single point of failure of DNS system would be avoided. Additionally, inbuilt characteristics of blockchain such as security, immutability also provides storage and logging of DNS records secured and temper-proof in distributed environment and these results in security of DNS system among common DNS threats and attacks such as Cache Poisoning and Spoofing & Hijacking Mitigation apart from DDoS attacks.

Ali et al., 2016 This paper represented an experimental detail of large-scale deployment of decentralized PKI on Namecoin blockchain. Namecoin is an experimental open-source framework that improves security, privacy and authorization of DNS and DNS participants in decentralized ecosystem by using blockchain technology [48]. In this paper, authors tried to expand this research by implementing PKI infrastructure over this built in Namecoin's blockchain based DNS infrastructure globally. Moreover, authors also discussed challenges and improvements faced during this global experiment. And how this global experience led to design of blockchain based naming and storage system especially for DNS named Blockstack. This proposed system Blockstack is launched as open-source project, and its PKI infrastructure serves around 55000 users in production that authors claimed in this paper. Additionally, authors try to fulfill security challenges found in Namecoin by implementing a Virtualchain Layer over Namecoin blockchain. This Virtualchain Layer responsible for extracting order information and operations from blocks which provides Blockstack capability to interact with Namecoin blockchain. System Architecture of Blockstack consists of Name operations (Control plane) and Content storage (Data plane). The Name Operations are responsible for initiating blockchain name->value transaction, verifies sequence of operations, verifies the block, stores these name data into name database and consensus and ordering task also handle by this Name Operations. The client resolution and off-chain storage of large name data are handled by Content storage. By evaluating performance matrix of Blockstack, it is stated that proposed system provides comparable performance to storage system with cost of slight overhead of CPU. This Blockstack PKI infrastructure tested for over 1 year when it deployed over Namecoin, provide high scalability and comparative performance to name storage system.

Kalodner et al., 2015 This comparative study focuses on Namecoin [48], a decentralized DNS, a public Proof-of-Work based blockchain DNS system and some key lessons for future's perspective while designing decentralized CDN system. In this paper, authors represent empirical study of Namecoin found some inactive systems in Namecoin's ecosystem. From this study, authors found mere 28 domains names are not squatted and holds low legitimate content among 120,000 registered domains names in Namecoin ecosystem. Additionally, transfer of domain detection technique especially designed for Namecoin blockchain, is key contribution of this research work. Some properties such as scarcity, transferability, expiration, low-friction registration, and robustness to sybil attacks are defined significant requirement of decentralized Namespace. In this empirical study, authors used on-chain metadata, DNS probs, content inspection techniques to filter out the active, parked, squatted, or unused domain names registered on Namecoin. This proposed model is Squatting Prevalence, user centric and robust model that detects domains names to provide good user experience and security of name record by leveraging blockchain technology. Some key suggestions for futuristic decentralized DNS design should include flexible incentive scheme, light weight client integration, and graceful expiration are briefly defined in this paper.

Li et al., 2021 A secure and efficient blockchain based DNS(B-DNS) system presented in this paper which tried to solve the problems of blockchain based DNS system such as computationally expensive Proof-of-Work (PoW) and an index of domain while building Proof-of-Stack protocol. Additionally, authors proposed a quantitative technique that compared security of legacy DNS and B-DNS by considering various factors such as attack cost, attack surface, and success ratio of attacks. B-DNS built on top of a Private Proof-of-Stack blockchain, that configure consensus for DNS registries. By introducing this custom Proof-of-Stack consensus mechanism, authors can get rid of computational heavy Proof-of-Work consensus protocol, which provides efficiency and flexibility to proposed model. Blockchain nodes run by all the participated Name servers (Registry Nodes), and responsible to store full ledger of domain registry, that prevents single point of failure risk in distributed system as it backed by blockchain. Smart contracts governed Domain registration, updates, and revocations processes in B-DNS system. For efficient and fast searching records on-chain, A domain-index Merkle tree was maintained which helps to lookup records directly through local chain in logarithmic time. Proof-of-Stack based B-DNS system efficiently improve security standards as sybil and Proof-of-Stack attacks become costly to implement on proposed system. Authors claimed that probability of successful attack on B-DNS is only 1% compared to a legacy DNS system because of this Proof-of-Stack based system implemented in B-DNS system. This proposed system is also efficiently processing query as its query performance evaluation is almost like existing commercial DNS Systems.

Xia et al., 2021 In this paper, authors present a large-scale experiential study of Ethereum Name Service (ENS) by evaluating numerous numbers of logs and on-chain event and recognized some patterns related to ENS adoption and its misuse for various purposes. In this study, authors evaluated that ENS system become highly acceptable during its initial four years because of distributed nature, open-source contributions and backed by blockchain's inbuilt characteristics. Authors also deeply studied and various security threat in traditional DNS system and Blockchain based ENS system (mainly focused on ENS smart contracts vulnerabilities). It is found that as open nature of ENS tends to more security risk for ENS systems. High adoption trends of ENS system, flexibility with various DNS record types and Fee Model & Auctions are the main characteristic of ENS system that elaborately defined in the paper. On Contrary, ENS system security side various ENS threats such as Name Squatting, spoofed addresses & phishing, smart contracts vulnerabilities are briefly discussed with its countermeasures. Result and analysis of this empirical study highlights some key statistics regarding number of active domains over total register domains, Squatting Name domain analysis, ENS renewal rates. By exploring deep analysis of security concern of blockchain based DNS, authors suggested a requirement of developing efficient threats mitigation system that can detect and mitigate security issues in Blockchain based DNS.

2.2.4. Smart contract-based approach for attack information filtering and sharing

Smart contracts is a piece of code, runs on blockchain which executes by itself(self-execution) when specific predefined conditions occurred. By introducing this smart contract, it eliminates requirements for central party or any intermediatory for contract invocation, transaction processing in secured, immutable, and transparent way especially in distributed system. As smart contracts execute on blockchain, blockchain's built in properties are automatically inherited in smart contracts such as temper-proof data logging, transparency and security. These smart contracts play significant role in DDoS attacks mitigation by attack information sharing and filtering. Additionally, self-executing property of smart contracts makes it perfect choice when introducing a collaborative solution in distributed and decentralized ecosystem. Smarts contracts are used for attack information or attack signature sharing among various peers in distributed network transparently, securely in automated way. Smart contracts are integrated with various attack detection or IDS for efficiently attack sharing and filtering in distributed systems. Some Smart contract-based key contributions for DDoS attack mitigation are analysed and discussed in this sub-section.

Authors	Years	Key Area covered	Utilization of Blockchain
(Patel & Patel, 2022)	2022	Blockchain, Reputation System, DDoS mitigation, IP reputation system	Smart contract used to store attack data, Polygon blockchain
(Xiong & Xiong, 2020)	2020	Smart contracts, Blockchain, Data protection	Ethereum blockchain, smart contracts for data protection and logs
(Panigrahi et al., 2023)	2023	DDoS mitigation, PKI, blockchain	Blockchain based PKI infrastructure
(Han et al., 2020)	2020	DDoS detection, collaborative detection scheme	Blockchain based collaborative approach, smart contracts, consortium blockchain
(Essaid et al., 2019)	2019	Deep Learning, RNN-LSTM, blockchain	Blockchain used for attack signaling, Ethereum Blockchain, AS

[Table 2.6: Literature Review – Smart contract-based approach for DDoS attacks Mitigation]

Patel & Patel, 2022 In this paper, authors represented a blockchain based DDoS attacks mitigation approach, which is collaborative in nature. Along with that IP reputation system is also defined in this paper. By utilizing blockchain for collaborative DDoS attack mitigation, authors leveraged inbuilt characteristics of blockchain technology such as transparency, security integrity and immutability in their distributed blockchain based DDoS attack mitigation solution. In this paper, blockchain is used for signaling the attack to other collaborators, means sharing attack information and blacklisted IP addresses to other participating peers improve attack prevention and detection for other collaborators' end. Authors also proposed IP reputation scheme that provide ratings to blacklisted IP addresses that improves accuracy and integrity of attack information. This accuracy in blacklisted IP address data not only detects DDoS attacks but also provide protection against other IP address related attacks on networks. This conceptual paper briefly discussed various Collaborative and Non-Collaborative DDoS attack mitigation approaches with IP reputation systems. Also shaded light on problems of Existing blockchain based collaborative DDoS mitigation solutions such as authentication, accuracy of attack data etc. Moreover, authors briefly discussed proposed system architecture which contains several components such as blockchain layer and Internal layer. Blockchain layer is responsible for executing smart contracts, communicate with decentralized storage system and integration with internal system. Whereas Internal layer mainly handled DDoS attack detection and mitigation task along with invocation of various smart contacts. Third-party IP reputation providers or public IP reputation providers are responsible for providing reputation score to blacklisted IP addresses in the proposed system. And based on this IP reputation score, Intrusion Prevention System (IPS) and IDS of proposed system blocked the blacklisted IP addresses. In this proposed system, Polygon, layer 2 blockchain is used for scalability and efficiency. Implementation and experimentation details of proposed system are not provided in this paper. But by evaluating this paper, this proposed blockchain based collaborative DDoS attack mitigation solution is scalable, secured and efficient and backed by blockchain to provide efficient solution in distributed attack mitigation space.

Xiong & Xiong, 2020 This paper proposed blockchain based framework that secured data selling and reselling processes in distributed ecosystem and main purpose behind this is preemption of unauthorized resale and usage of data resources by leveraging inbuilt features of blockchain technology. In this paper, data-for-share mechanism is introduced by using Ethereum blockchain and smart contracts for prevention of data resources reselling and misusage. Authors proposed large-margin multi-task metric learning to resolve disputes in data-for-sale disputes. As well as introduced some algorithms especially for data source protection such as assess to market, dispute resolution algorithms etc. In this proposed framework, smart contracts are utilized for management of data access permissions at various stages of these algorithms. And blockchain provides central registry to store and log immutable, temper-proof data across various collaborators in distributed space. Data source protection though data-for-sale and dispute resolution mechanisms briefly defined in this paper. Here, smart contracts become medium to share trade details securely with various participating peers in trading of data. Smart contracts implementation details are also provided. By combining blockchain and smart contracts enhances overall system performance and security where blockchain acts as central logging repository with smart contracts automates transaction processing and enhance security by introducing automated access control and mitigate risk of unauthorized data trading.

Panigrahi et al., 2023 In this paper, authors present a blockchain based PKI especially for Certificate management automation. PKI is a backbone of user authentication and communication processes. The traditional PKI has many loopholes such as single point of failure as its centralized nature, high latency, deficient authentication processes for certificate creation, verification and certificate authority related security threats. By considering all the drawbacks of conventional mechanism, blockchain based PKI become first choice in community as it combines Log based PKI (LBPKI), Web of Trust (WoT) mechanisms of PKI. In this paper, authors designed a lightweight PKI by choosing blockchain based approach along with introduced a lightweight smart contract with less storage capacity especially designed for lightweight applications. Introduced threshold value in smart contracts that defined a limit for a participating node to become Certificate authority (CA). These smart contracts are designed by considering security in a center so as a result prevention of many cyber-attacks on PKI infrastructure possible. From implementation perspective, this proposed solution is deployed on Ethereum blockchain with Geth client. By considering lightweight application perspective, in proposed system design leveraged Delegated Proof of Stake (DPoS) consensus algorithm as efficiently implement high scalable and low latency solution. Certificate issuance, validation, and revocation processes are implemented through Solidity based Smart contracts for efficient and secured automation of Certificate related operations. Here smart contracts are introduced to shared Certificate Authority (CA) PKI related transaction processes among all the participating peers. In proposed system, all the participating nodes are free to choose their own certificate authority (CA), this flexible design choice defined implementation of Web of Trust (WoT) model. By evaluating result statistics, it is stated that proposed blockchain based solution achieved high scalability, security and efficiency (low latency for certificate creation and verification processes) in PKI infrastructure especially for lightweight applications.

Han et al., 2020 The decentralized DDoS attacks detection framework is presented by implementing blockchain because of decentralized nature of blockchain for attack mitigation. By inspired from Biological immune system, authors built this collaborative blockchain based framework that detect and respond the DDoS attacks in adaptive and self-learning manner. Adaptive and self-learning are two fundamental characteristics of Biological immune system, by implementing these properties in DDoS attack detection mechanism, provide efficient and real time DDoS attack detection in decentralized Ecosystem. By implementing blockchain technology for collaborative solution, it offered transparency, immutability, security and co-ordination among different collaborators of the system. To design this proposed framework, consortium blockchain is implemented as management of all the collaborators participated in single private chain. For privacy preserving design, each participants wise a private blockchain allocated. In this proposed framework, smart contracts are responsible for detect and share DDoS attacks data to other peers and generate anonymous chain for each participating organization's network. By distributing attacks detection work among multiple organizations (collaborators), this proposed system achieved high resilience against this distributed attacks and risk of single point of failure of collaborator's node in distributed system is also avoided. Because of adaptive nature of proposed system, attack detection accuracy is going to increased significantly over time. Blockchain and smart contracts-based system design provided high security and transparency to attack information along with decentralized co-ordination in un-trusted environment.

Essaid et al., 2019 In this paper, authors proposed a collaborative DDoS attacks mitigation framework that leveraged blockchain technology and deep learning approach for efficient attack mitigation. Requirements of Collaborative mitigation solution are briefly discussed, and available collaborative solutions are costly and increased implementation complexity. So blockchain technology become ideal choice to design collaborative mitigation solution as distributed nature of blockchain, transparency, security, auditability, and immutability. In Autonomous System (As) level, blockchain technology mainly utilized for signaling attacks and collaborative resource sharing during attacks. A deep learning approaches, a Recurrent Neural Network with Long Short-Term Memory (RNN-LSTM) mainly analyzed network traffic, searched out anomalies and detect attack traffic from overall system traffic. This proposed framework, after detection of attack, filtered out attack traffic from the normal traffic, and only blocked the attacks traffic so normal traffic sourced from the attack route would be served without any interruption, that the core functionality of this framework. Here, Ethereum smart contracts leveraged as medium to share attack information and mitigation strategies to other participating AS through Ethereum blockchain. When attack traffic detected smart contracts are automatically invoked and shared signaling of attack data to all the collaborators over blockchain. By evaluating result statistics, this proposed framework achieved high detection accuracy as based on RNN-LSTM model and high scalability and flexibility with efficient collaboration through blockchain technology.

2.3. Collaborative DDoS attacks Mitigation without implementing Blockchain based Infrastructure

In Collaborative DDoS attacks Mitigation, attack prevention, detection, defence and mitigation are performed collaboratively by group of organizations or networks who share same interest in terms of DDoS attack Mitigation. Idea of collaborative attack mitigation originated from distributed nature of DDoS attacks. All the organizations involved in Collaboration process might be either trusted or untrusted to each other. But majority of Collaborations are formed where Collaborators come from untrusted environments. One of the main challenges in Collaborative DDoS attack mitigation is to establish trust and transparency between different collaborators belongs to untrusted environments. For that central party or community organization is created whose responsibility involves enforce transparent and trustworthy collaboration process. Additionally, establishment of rules and regulations for attack detection, prevention and mitigation are also complex task which jointly handle by central authority and all the collaborators. Implementation of collaborative mitigation solution is complex. There are various network level and infrastructure level complexities are involved while design such type of solution. Moreover, authenticity and trust of shared data is biggest challenge in collaborative attacks mitigation solution.

To address these challenges, Blockchain technology is ideal choice, as its decentralized nature to form trust in untrusted environment, transparency, security, immutability. As result, majority of collaborative solutions utilize blockchain to design collaborative solution. But in this section, we discussed several collaborative DDoS attacks mitigation solutions without implementing blockchain based architecture that implemented various strategies such as SDN,

Client-server architecture to build collaborations of peers for attack prevention, detection, mitigation in untrusted environment.

Authors	Years	Key Area covered	Collaboration mechanism used
(Hameed & Ahmed Khan, 2018)	2018	SDN, Controller to controller communication protocol	Controller to controller communication protocol
(Moriarty, 2012)	2012	PKI, incidence handling data	Consortium and PKI based infrastructure, XML messages
(Boucadair et al., 2022)	2022	DOTS protocol Enhancement, attack detection, mitigation, Collaborative approach,	Used Client-Server Architecture, Collaborative
(Rashidi & Fung, 2016)	2016	Virtual Network Function, DDoS mitigation, Resource allocation problem	Using Network Function virtualization, Incentive Compatible approach
(Bremler-Barr & Sabag, 2022)	2022	Information protocol, Routing, Filters, Collaborative approach	By implementing DDoS Open Threat Signaling Protocol (DOTS)
(Tayfour & Marsono, 2021)	2021	SDN, Collaborative approach, attack mitigation, an ensemble classifier	SDN, multiple-controller domain collaboration, through RSMQM mechanism

[Table 2.7: Literature Review – Collaborative DDoS attacks Mitigation solutions without implementing Blockchain based Infrastructure]

Hameed & Ahmed Khan, 2018 Authors represented a collaborative DDoS mitigation solution by leveraging SDN among various AS. A brief discussion about SDN, its two components control plane and data plane are also provided. In this paper, authors designed a Controller-to-Controller(C-to-C), a communication protocol especially worked on SDN controller level of various AS. This C-to-C protocol is a core of collaboration logic in SDN domain for this proposed system architecture, that securely communicate and share attack signatures between various AS. In C-to-C protocol, special payload for message exchange was also designed, it contained Data section that stored IP address and attack signatures whereas Certificate section contained security certificate data and signature section stored message digest signed by private key of security certificate. The controller modules are combination of three different modules named Policy listener module, Payload verification module, Policy pusher module, responsible for implementing controller level functionalities. This centralized SDN based collaborative solution aimed to block attack traffic near source of attack network and repetition of attack detection and mitigation tasks for various collaborators. This proposed framework tested by deploying it over various deployment model such as linear, central, and mesh. Based on these experimental results, this proposed SDN based collaborative framework is efficient, scalable and fast in collaborative DDoS attacks mitigation across multiple SDN based domains.

Moriarty, 2012 Request for Comments (RFC) 6545 published by the Internet Engineering Task Force (IETF) defined a standardized framework named Real-time Inter-network Defense (RID) for the purpose of transmitting cybersecurity incident information between various organizations. Author proposed a dynamic communication mechanism especially designed for inter-network communication that share real time incident-handling data across organizations boundaries. RID framework provides incident handling service by integrating with existing detection, mitigation, tracing, source identification services of participating organizations(collaborators). Through this proposed framework achieved higher security levels on networks. For the purpose of efficient communication between Computer Security Incident Response Teams (CSIRTs) and service providers (collaborators) in collaborative way, a special XML based message format for incident information was designed named Incident Object Description Exchange Format (IODEF). RID used extension of this IODEF for real time incident-handling data transmission between collaborators. This extended version of IODEF supports multiple message types such as Request, Acknowledgement, Result, Report and Query. RID enforced Policy-based sharing mechanism that represented terms and conditions of incident data sharing between collaborators, that brings transparency and trust in collaboration process. Various relationship model for collaborators communications such as Client-To-SP (Client-To-Service Providers), SP-To-Client (Service Providers-To-Client), Peer-To-Peer, Intra-Consortium and Between Consortiums defined communication types of collaborators. For secure message communication, secure communication channels are designed that implemented security through authentication, and encrypted channels (e.g., HTTP over TLS) to fulfill data security and integrity requirements. RID's communication mechanism built on Client-Server mechanism for coordinate detection, tracing and attack identification so risk of single point of failure of communication servers involved.

Additionally, from implementation perspective proposed framework arises implementation complexity and introduces various integration challenges for collaborator's networks.

Boucadair et al., 2022 Request for Comments (RFC) 9244 published by the Internet Engineering Task Force (IETF) is enhancement of Distributed Denial-of-Service Open Threat Signaling (DOTS) protocol for DDoS attacks mitigation through exchange of attack data between participating parties in DOTS collaboration. DOTS protocol exchanges information about network resources and network state of DOTS Client to DOTS Servers (capable of providing network resources to under-attack DOTS Clients) and DOTS server provides attack mitigation by sharing network resources and other mitigation strategies in response. Authors enhanced DOTS protocol by including signal channels with various telemetry attributes, for the purpose of optimal DDoS attacks mitigation in collaborative ecosystem. When DOTS client sends mitigation request to DOTS server, attributes such as Normal traffic baseline, attack traffic telemetry, mitigation efficacy telemetry are included in the attack mitigation request. In response to this mitigation request, DOTS server includes mitigation status attribute in response to DOTS clients. These attributes play significant role in effective DDoS attacks mitigation and helpful for the mitigators to choose appropriate DDoS attack mitigation strategies. Collaboration between DOTS Clients and DOTS Server established through DOTS signal channels which utilized to share attack telemetry of data. These signal channels facilitated communication between DOTS Clients and DOTS Server, where DOTS client setup telemetry attributes such as Normal traffic baseline, attack traffic telemetry. DOTS Server responsible for sharing Mitigation Status and Efficacy Report to DOTS clients. Collaboration process includes several steps from Telemetry configuration to mitigation Activation and feedback loop. Telemetry messages are being serialized by using Concise Binary Object Representation (CBOR) for efficient message delivery and error handling over network. From security point of view, all DOTS messages must be encrypted and authenticated. Detailed implementation details of this DOTS enhancement are given from infrastructure setup to message types. This DOTS Enhancement efficiently mitigate DDoS attacks in collaborative space through enhanced visibility into network traffic and continuous adjustment in attack mitigation strategies. Here, for collaboration Client-Server mechanism is used for attack signaling and mitigation communication between various collaborative organizations, which leads to single point of failure problem. This proposed protocol is also complex to implement and has its own implementation challenges.

Rashidi & Fung, 2016 In this paper, authors presented a collaborative framework named CoFence, that collaboratively detects DDoS attack especially SYN floods in Network Function Virtualization (NVF) based domains. This proposed framework collaboratively mitigate DDoS attacks by sharing unused network resources among other NVF based domains (collaborators). By considering limitation of traditional DDoS mitigation solution, this proposed collaborative solution utilized NVF to design more flexible and low-cost mitigation solution. CoFence mainly address resource allocation problem of collaborative DDoS defense mechanism by designing a reciprocal-based utility function. In large scale DDoS attacks, this collaborative solution allows NVF-based domains to distribute unused network resources to under-attack domain, that brings flexibility and resilience of overall system. In CoFence framework, a virtual Internet Service Provider (ISP) is enabled on each ISP or Enterprise Networks (collaborators) as this virtual ISP has capability of NFV. Trust management in collaboration established through a Service Agreement procedure, a process where all domains agree upon predetermined terms and service conditions. A virtual ISP is a central component through which collaboration among various NVF based domains managed. This a virtual ISP has two main components: communication component, through communication between different virtual IPS possible, and Resource allocation component, whose responsibility to share requested resources to under-attack domain. In CoFence framework, the reciprocal-based resource assignment mechanism mainly introduced for cooperations and collaboration between NVF based domain while ongoing DDoS attacks. By considering the simulation results of proposed framework, authors stated that proposed solution is effective, impartial, and Incentive Compatible solution that efficiently addressed the problem of resource allocation in collaborative ecosystem.

Bremler-Barr & Sabag, 2022 Motivation behind this research is increasing DDoS attacks especially reflection denial of service attacks (DRDoS) in internet ecosystem because of IP spoofing (Source IP spoofing). Due to lack of monetary rewards mechanism, many commercial organizations avoid this IP spoofing prevention mechanism while design a new DDoS mitigation solution. In this paper, authors tried to provide solution of DRDoS attacks by introducing an economical incentive mechanism in route-based defense technique especially for mitigating risk of source IP spoofing. This paper presented a collaborative on-demand route-based defense technique (CORB) for providing DDoS mitigation as a paid-for-service.

Additionally, CORB efficiently suppressed the attack traffic before the traffic reflected by the reflector or overwhelmed the victim network. Overall, CORB technique efficiently reduced the intensity of DDoS attacks near the source of attack, as result victim network function normally after eliminating risk of reflection attacks. In this technique, authors utilized the internet service providers (ISPs) and internet exchange points (IXPs) widespread across all over internet to filter out small portion traffic data (border gateway protocol (BGP) based data) of victim network through scrubbing. Here scrubbing facility is core technique that trace traffic data, reach to its original source, and discarding malicious and attack traffic, mainly used by scrubbing center of ISP. For communication between victim network and scrubbing centers of ISP, this proposed technique utilized built-in protocol named DOTS (DDoS Open Threat Signaling) protocol, a DDoS attacks signaling protocol developed by the Internet Engineering Task Force (IETF). This scrubbing centers of ISP receives monetary incentives as become part of DDoS attack mitigation by filtering the victim's traffic. By introducing DDoS mitigation as a paid-for-service for attack victim networks (collaborator) and incentivize the scrubbing centers (collaborator) for filtrations of attack traffic, proposed CORB technique become manually beneficial to all parties involved in DDoS mitigation. This CORB technique is evaluated by simulating a Memcached DRDoS attack using real-life time data. Based on result statistics, it is stated that proposed framework is efficient, cost-effective and flexible solution to mitigate DRDoS attacks.

Tayfour & Marsono, 2021 In this paper, authors proposed framework that collaboratively detect and mitigate DDoS attacks in SDN. Authors briefly discussed DDoS attacks againts SDN controller and OpenFolw switch as core domains of SDN. As part of this proposed framework, three key modules are introduced based upon its role in DDoS mitigation process. In first module named classifier module deployed an ensemble classifier, Voting-based Nonparametric Kernel Density Estimation (V-NKDE) for attack detection accuracy. The second module, the mitigation module responsible for blocking illegitimate traffic after attack detection and eradicating these entries from flow-table for avoid transmitting attacks traffic within the network as prevention measures. The collaborative module mainly performed collaboration between multiple SDN controllers by transmitting attack detection and mitigation flow table rules through Redis Simple Message Queue mechanism (RSMQM) among different SDN controllers(collaborators). This collaborative module built inter-SDN based controller collaboration through that effective DDoS attack defense and mitigation strategy designed and implemented over multiple SDN based domains. Various standardized datasets such as nSDN2020, CICIDS2017, NSL-KDD and UNSW-NB15 along with real time SDN simulation utilized for validating performance of Classifier module (attack detection accuracy). Based on result statistics of these experiments, authors stated that proposed framework achieved high attack detection accuracy with V-NKDE classifier compared to single classifier. And reduction in false positive rate, significantly reduced controller overhead for coordinating attack detection and mitigation across multiple SDN based controller. Because of collaboration mechanism introduced between multiple SDN based controller, efficient resource utilization of network resources becomes possible and significantly reduced risk of single point of failure in SDN ecosystem.

2.4. Non-Collaborative DDoS attack Mitigation using Blockchain based Infrastructure

Because of distributed nature of blockchain, serve it as a complete solution for collaborative domains to establish trust, transparency and security in untrusted environment. Majority of collaborative solutions leverages Blockchain technology because of its inbuilt properties that reduce need of complex infrastructure and centralized trust authority. But apart from that, Contribution of blockchain technology in non-collaborative DDoS mitigation is also considerable. There are various solutions which utilized blockchain technology in non-collaborative ways involves IoT based solutions, Smart contract-based solutions and machine learning integrated solutions. As blockchain technology enables by default data integrity, transparency with infrastructure, it eliminates requirements for enforcement of additional infrastructure resources and is cost-effective, for this reason, non-collaborative solutions integrate blockchain technology to design their solutions. Some non-collaborative blockchain integrated solutions are discussed in this sub-section.

Authors	**Years**	**Key Area covered**	**Utilization of Blockchain**
(Arachchige et al., 2024)	2024	IoT, IoT sensor network, DDoS mitigation, Anomaly detection	Authentication and authorization, provides immutability to network activity logs,

(Issam Aljanabi et al., 2022)	2022	Detection and mitigation of attack, Reverse connection requests techniques, Round-robbing load distribution	Smart contract-based blacklist sharing, immutable logging, single point of failure resolution
(Yakubu et al., 2023)	2023	colluding attacks prevention, Smart home device to device authentication system, Single server queuing system model	Ethereum blockchain and Smart contracts for authentication, monitoring and logging
(Kumari et al., 2024)	2024	Machine learning, Blockchain technology, IoT, Random Forest model, attack detection and mitigation	To store blacklisted IP & timestamps recorded on Blockchain, authentication of IoT devices, temper proof stored data
(Jmal et al., 2023)	2023	Attack detection and mitigation, ANN, IoT, SDN based multi-controllers	Facilitate secure communication between multiple SDN controllers, maintained data integrity, auditing and traceability

[Table 2.8: Literature Review – Non-Collaborative DDoS attacks Mitigation solutions using Blockchain based Infrastructure]

Arachchige et al., 2024 In this paper, authors evaluated utilization of Blockchain technology in IoT networks as a mitigation solution of DDoS attacks. Potential of blockchain technology to secure resource-constrained IoT environment against DDoS attacks and possible security vulnerabilities of blockchain technology as a solution to mitigate DDoS attacks are also briefly discussed in this paper. In this paper, this proposed low-powered IoT sensor networks framework is integrated with three different blockchains such as Hydrachain, Monero, Duino coin, and gathered experimental results. In this research, blockchain technology is leveraged to increase security of IoT sensor networks by providing data integrity and security of IoT data in resource constrained IoT sensor networks, along with that single point of failure problem also resolved automatically as decentralized nature of blockchain technology. To design real time testbed different hardware device such as Raspberry Pi devices, Orange Pi Zero 2 along with various software such as Wireshark, DSTAT, MPSTAT and different blockchains related resources were used. Based on these results statistics, authors stated that DDoS attacks against this blockchain powered resource-constrained IoT sensor networks resulted in considerable anomalies in network and system performance. Additionally, average increase in CPU core usage to 34.32%, up to 66% decrease in hash rates, batch timeout increased to 14.25% and block latency increased to 11.1% are noticed. These findings are indicator of potential of blockchain technology in DDoS attack mitigation in such type of IoT networks.

Issam Aljanabi et al., 2022 This paper presented solution to mitigate DDoS attacks especially TCP attacks by leveraging blockchain technology and reverse connection requests techniques for Bot identification. For identification of legitimacy of IP address, by utilizing reverse request technique, system send reverse request to the incoming request's IP address, if response comes then it considers as legitimate IP otherwise puts this IP in blacklisted IP category. After that this blacklisted IP addresses stored in blacklist maintained by smart contracts so that this list becomes accessible to all the peers. To distribute traffic to among auxiliary nodes when network capacity reached at threshold, round robin mechanism was used for efficient load balancing and maintain detection accuracy in distributed network. In this paper, blockchain technology is used for multiple purposes such as to resolve problem of single point of failure in distributed network, smart contracts-based blacklist sharing, and immutable records of network activities for logging and monitoring. Main benefit of this TCP based attacks mitigation approach is to prevent network failure and uninterrupted service delivery to end-users. After experimental implementation of this proposed framework, authors stated that attack detection rate and accuracy of attacks detection were above 99%, with significant lower false positive rates and false alarm rates. Additionally, by achieving high attack detection matrix, proposed farmwork took around 0.749 seconds to find out attacking address that reveals high system performance with high detection accuracy of proposed system.

Yakubu et al., 2023 In this paper, authors tried to resolve authentication problem of smart Homes's device while device to device communication. Security threats in smart home network leads to numerous cyber-attacks and security risk especially possibility of a colluding attacks (DDoS attacks over smart home network in simple terms). To resolve this problem, authors introduced a lightweight authentication mechanism for secure Device to Device communication in smart home network. In this proposed framework, Ethereum blockchain is utilized to implement distributed prototype and to leverage other functionalities of blockchain. DDoS attacks mitigation actions performed in this proposed framework by controlling service request through authentication and single server queuing system. Implementation of Single server queuing system model in proposed system aimed to prevent resource exhaustion while DDoS attacks by managing incoming requests, directing concurrent requests in system. In this research, Ethereum smart contracts were employed for authentication process over blockchain, that eliminated need for central authentication server (also resolved problem of single point of failure of authentication server). Moreover, authentication mechanism handled by blockchain in proposed system, facilitated smart home devices' communication secure, reliable and reduced overhead of authentication on individual devices. Additionally, all authentication transactions are recorded on chain, so these on chain data utilized for further analysis, logging and monitoring. In proposed system implementation, simulation was performed on multiple devices for 20 times, aimed to quantify system consistency over various type of devices. After considering this simulation results, authors stated that proposed system successfully prevent and mitigate DDoS attacks (colluding attacks) over smart home networks and outperformed the existing protocols in terms of message processing, computational cost and response time, this shows effectiveness of this proposed framework in IoT ecosystem.

Kumari et al., 2024 By leveraging machine learning and blockchain technology for DDoS attacks detection in IoT ecosystem is core idea of this research study. This proposed solution detects DDoS attacks real time though machine learning algorithm then after attack detection details especially malicious IP addresses stored over blockchain. In this paper, authors used Proof of Work (PoW) blockchain to provide immutability, integrity, reliability and correctness of stored blacklisted data without having third-party for logging and monitoring purposes. Additionally, decentralized nature of blockchain provided efficient way to authenticate IoT devices without establishing central authentication entity. Various security policies and rules such as access control, real time vulnerability detection were enforced in proposed system by invoking smart contracts. After Machine learning model detected the attacks, predefined mitigation strategies such as isolating malicious nodes, rerouting traffic, ensuring automated responses were implemented through smart contract invocation. Sepolia TestNet, official TestNet of Ethereum is utilized to implement blockchain and Solidity smart contracts. For evaluating performance of proposed system, various datasets such as CSE-CIC-IDS2018AWS, CICIDS2017, and CICDoS2016 were employed for effectiveness of proposed system. By evaluating various machine learning algorithms for proposed system model, authors stated that the Random Forest model achieved highest accuracy of 99.34%, and overperformed other models. As result of this, proposed system also achieved high accuracy in DDoS attacks detection and gained high data immutability and security through blockchain based architecture. Moreover, overall system latency was also reduced as mitigation strategy enforced through intermediate smart contracts over multiple IoT networks. Proposed system achieved high scalability as authentication of increasing number of IoT devices handled by blockchain technology.

Jmal et al., 2023 In this paper, author briefly discussed DDoS attacks on IoT domains and DDoS attacks on SDN domains. Additionally, A systematic review of blockchain based, SDN based, and machine learning based various DDoS attacks detection, mitigation techniques and mechanism were given in this paper. Authors proposed a multi-controllers SDN based IoT system, also integrated blockchain and ANN for efficient attacks detection and mitigation in IoT ecosystem. In this proposed framework, blockchain ensured security and immutability in distributed SDN based IoT networks and efficient attack detection, mitigation performed by ANN. A brief review of SDN capabilities to mitigate DDoS attacks on IoT domains and blockchain technology to enhance SDN security also provided in this paper. In this proposed system, SDN separates data plane from control plane, so it provides centralized control over network through control plane management. It enabled traffic management, rules management, dynamic reconfiguration, that effective for attacks detection and mitigation in proposed system. Moreover, firewall integration with data plane, prevented illegitimate traffic in network, and encryption of data reduced risk of various cyber-attacks such as unauthorized access, data tampering. ANN detected attacks traffic by analyzing network traffic patterns and anomalies detection. Along with that ANN also adapted to new attack mitigation rules and strategies as has learning ability. Blockchain enabled secure, immutable communication between various SDN controllers, that enhanced reliability of communication data in IoT networks. additionally, as distributed nature of blockchain, mitigate risk of central point of failure of SDN domains, by assuring SDN flow rules and policies were controlled by multiple SDN based domains. As security events and data recorded over blockchain, provided secure and immutable logging and monitoring. By evaluating the experimental result of proposed framework, it is stated that the ANN based detection of proposed system detects attacks with high accuracy. Integration of blockchain with multi-controller SDN based IoT systems efficiently mitigate

DDoS attacks as blockchain enables sharing of mitigation flow rules and strategies effectively among multiple SDN controllers that reduced system latency in attacks detection and mitigation. Additionally, proposed system achieved high scalability and Resilience because of integration of blockchain and multiple-SDN based IoT systems.

2.5. Motivation of Research / Objectives of Research

There are various DDoS Mitigation strategies and solutions used in market. Different types of DDoS attacks demand various mitigation strategies and solutions. Additionally, Utilization of Blockchain technology in DDoS attacks mitigation space is still in initial phase. Blockchain Technology has great potential to be utilized as a solution to mitigate DDoS attack in terms of attack prevention, detection and mitigation. Blockchain has built in features such as transparency, security, immutability opts it as a perfect choice to design a solution which falls under category of Collaborative DDoS attack Mitigation as nature of Blockchain is distributed and decentralized by default.

- Main motivation behind this research is to design a solution which serve as a key solution in collaborative DDoS attack Mitigation by utilizing Blockchain technology.
- Desing a collaborative and distributed solution that deal with volumetric DDoS attacks in distributed manner as nature of attack, most efficient way to mitigate volumetric DDoS attacks.
- Repeatedly Volumetric attack detection and mitigation should be avoided as nature of solution distributed and collaborative.
- Designing a blockchain based solution which integrate with any existing network detection and mitigation with minimal configuration.
- Block attack traffic near the source of the attack, so that Attack traffic should not traverse to other intermediate domains.

2.6 Research Questions / Research Hypothesis

The main motive behind this research is to design a collaborative mitigation solution that build transparency, trust and security between untrusted domains by implementing blockchain based solution. Along with that mitigate Volumetric DDoS attacks by using smart contract oriented blockchain based collaborative solution in distributed and decentralized manner. So, the main objectives of this research work are to build transparent collaboration process and to design blockchain based collaborative mitigation solution. As nature of DDoS attack is distributed, so distributed mitigation solution becomes prominent in DDoS mitigation ecosystem.

To fulfill these objectives, we have defined the following targets:

1. This blockchain based solution provides transparency, security, and authenticity to share attack information among all the collaborators without implementing any specialized infrastructure.
2. Implementing this mitigation solution, will significantly enhance attack detection and mitigation capability of other collaborative domains.
3. As result of this collaborative solution, repeatedly attack detection and mitigation tasks will be avoided.
4. By implementing this blockchain based collaborative solution, Volumetric DDoS attack mitigation will be performed collaboratively and distributed manner.
5. Volumetric DDoS attack traffic will be blocked near source of attack, significantly improves other domains performance.

2.7 Research Contribution / Importance of Research

The significance of this research work can be recognized as followings:

- This blockchain based solution provides significant contribution in Collaborative DDoS attack mitigation space.
- Avoiding repetition attack detection and mitigation work in collaborative domains
- Transparent attack detection and mitigation
- Secured, transparent and accurate attack information sharing between untrusted collaborative domains without any third party
- This blockchain based solution integrates with existing mitigation system with no to minimal configuration.

- Distributed blockchain based solution to deal with Volumetric DDoS attack that distributed in nature.
- Resource optimization (Gas optimization) in attack information storage and transmission.
- Helpful to mitigate some common network threats such as IP based attacks (Spamming, port scanning, Man-in-the-Middle attack) indirectly.

2.8 Limitation of the Research

This Blockchain based solution mainly contributes to provide DDoS mitigation solution for Collaborative DDoS attack Mitigation space, mainly in terms of collaboration, attack prevention and mitigation. This research does not provide its contribution in DDoS attack mitigation as a single domain. Additionally, in each domain of blockchain based collaboration are free to use its own attack detection and mitigation systems. Mainly attack detection and blocking is handled by individual domains according to its own network and security policy. Because to design a central attack detection and mitigation policy for all the collaborative domains would not be feasible and efficient and acceptable to each domain in network.

CHAPTER 3: RESEARCH METHODOLOGY

This research aims to mitigate volumetric DDoS attacks by implementing Blockchain based architecture collaboratively. The overall research methodology is discussed in this chapter. The entire research methodology for proposed system involves Collaborative DDoS mitigation approach, Blockchain selection, Blockchain based infrastructure (IPFS (Benet, 2014) and Smart contracts) and data generation.

3.1. Research Paradigm and Design

This proposed research follows Design Science Research (DSR) methodology (Brocke et al., 2020), that suitable for cyber-security, Blockchain and software engineering fields. DSR mainly involves creation, implementation and validation of novel frameworks and algorithms that aimed to solve real-world problems. In this proposed research, we designed a blockchain based architecture that collaboratively mitigate volumetric DDoS attacks. This research identifies challenges and problems of existing collaborative mitigation approach and tries to solve collaboration problem by employing secure and decentralized blockchain based architecture. This proposed blockchain based architecture was implemented by utilizing Smart contracts deployed over Polygon's official TestNet named Mumbai TestNet (polygonscan.com, n.d.) and for decentralized storage implemented by leveraging IPFS. This proposed solution was evaluated by simulating and emulating various volumetric DDoS attacks such as TCP, UDP and ICMP attacks towards Victim networks. And measured several metrics such as security behavior, performance of system and cost (transaction costs) for proposed system validation and evaluation purposes. Overall, this whole process of creation, testing and validation and evaluation of this proposed technological solution, directly defied the DSR approach.

Moreover, this proposed study also aligned with Applied research ("Applied Science," 2025), as proposed framework addressed and tried to solve real-world problem (practical problem) of collaborative mitigation approach of DDoS attacks by employing blockchain based infrastructure. This proposed solution provides deployable mitigation solution, deployed over Polygon's official TestNet, Mumbai TestNet and Decentralized application (DApp) rather than defining pure theoretical concepts. This proposed study is trying to provide efficient collaborative mitigation solution in DDoS attacks mitigation space.

Additionally, this proposed research studies falls under the category of Experimental Reasearch paradigm (Srinagesh, 2006) as experiment were conducted to validate and evaluate proposed framework. Simulation and emulation of volumetric DDoS attacks were conducted to validate and test proposed blockchain based architecture for collaborative attacks mitigation. These experiments were conducted on controlled testbed environment and under real network. Performance and various other metrics were carried out from these experiments and evaluated systematically.

In this proposed research study, these research methodologies and its combinations demonstrates innovation, practical applicability of proposed research, supported through systematic validation and evaluation.

3.2. Adoption of Collaborative DDoS Mitigation approach in Proposed System Design

As Distributed nature of DDoS attacks, attacks mitigation solution should be distributed in nature to efficiently mitigate DDoS attacks. Distributed attacks mitigation solutions not only mitigate DDoS attacks but also reduce risk of DDoS attacks on other networks. These are the main reasons why Collaborative DDoS Mitigation approach has become the first choice among research community and industry. In Collaborative DDoS attacks Mitigation, attack prevention, detection, defense and mitigation are performed collaboratively by group of organizations or networks (collaborators) who share same interest in terms of DDoS attack Mitigation. By combining capabilities of all the collaborators, efficiently mitigate DDoS attacks in distributed ecosystem. While designing a collaborative solution, a transparent and trustworthy collaboration must be the first condition. In majority of collaborative solutions, centralized third-party handle this responsibility. But implementation of collaboration solution arises challenges such as infrastructure level complexity, authentication of collaborators, authenticity of data. Additionally, single point of failure is biggest problem especially when collaboration process handles by single centralized entity.

On contrary, by default Blockchain technology establishes trust and transparency in untrusted distributed environment, which makes it perfect choice for collaborative mitigation solution design. Blockchain utilized for forming trust and transparency among various participating networks (Collaborators) belongs to untrusted environment without relying on centralized third-party. Moreover, blockchain technology's built-in characteristics such as security, immutability and transparency by default inherited in a collaborative attack mitigation solution.

The Proposed solution aimed to mitigate Volumetric DDoS attacks by leveraging Blockchain Technology. The proposed solution is designed by adopting collaborative DDoS attacks mitigation approach after considering significance of collaborative mitigation solution in DDoS attacks mitigation. As we discussed above, establishing a transparent and trustworthy collaboration process is biggest challenge, to solve this problem, blockchain technology is utilized for transparent collaboration process among various participating networks. In system design of proposed solution, collaborative approach is beneficial in attack detection, mitigation and prevention among collaborators' networks efficiently. In this collaboration process, blockchain technology provides infrastructure for transparent, trustworthy and secured collaboration process without intervene of third-party among different untrusted participating networks (collaborators). Additionally, secured and transparent authentication of collaborators, authenticity of data (attack signature data) are also handled through blockchain based infrastructure in this proposed system.

3.3. Selection of Blockchain for Proposed system design

The Proposed solution leveraged blockchain technology to resolve challenges raised to implement Collaborative mitigation approach for efficient attacks detection and mitigation in untrusted environment. In market various types of blockchains are available to serve different proposes and use cases. Public blockchains are mainly implemented where high transparency, open access of data and open participation of peers are highly preferred. On the other hand, Private blockchains are ideal for use cases where data privacy, speed of transactions and closed peer participation are mainly taken into consideration. Consortium blockchains are beneficial for scenarios where moderate decentralization and shared control are prominent requirements. In general, any of specific type does not fit in all the scenarios and use cases, so selection of blockchain for any use case always depends on tradeoffs between its prominent and obscure requirements.

In proposed system design, our prominent requirements are transparency, security and open collaboration among peers for the purpose of efficient Volumetric DDoS attacks mitigation. To fulfill these requirements of open, decentralized collaboration, we chose Public blockchain as it efficiently serves all the requirements by defaults. Again, Public blockchains contains many different sub-categories of blockchains such as based on consensus mechanism, based on functionality and based on Layer etc. These different categories serve different proposes and requirements like cryptocurrency-focused, interoperability platforms, smart contracts functionality and layers etc.

While selection of specific category of blockchain, different system requirements were taken into consideration and after meticulosity analyzed requirements, decision was made. In Proof of Stack consensus mechanism, validators (miners in PoW) are randomly choose based on amount of Stack (native crypto tokens holding) for block creation and transaction confirmation. PoS is energy efficient, scalable and mainly Economically Driven Secured mechanism compared to other consensus mechanism. Additionally, PoS based blockchains are widely adopted and tested and acquired vast community support. Secondly, Proposed system required Smart Contract for sharing attack information among collaborators. Smart contracts provide programmability and auto-invocation and efficient mechanism to interact with blockchain. By considering these requirements, Proof of Stack (PoS) and smart contracts based blockchains was ideal choice for system design. Because of PoS and Smart contracts requirements fulfillments, Ethereum (Ethereum Whitepaper, n.d.) and Polygon blockchain (Polygon, n.d.) was ideal choice for Proposed system.

In proposed system design, Ethereum was first choice as it fulfilled all the system requirements. But Ethereum blockchain faced some major challenges such as scalability, high transaction processing time and higher gas fees. By considering these challenges, we selected Polygon (Polygon, n.d.), a layer 2 scaling solution of Ethereum blockchain, for proposed system. As Polygon layer 2 solution of Ethereum, it efficiently solved scalability problem by processing transaction faster and cheaper compared to Ethereum. Moreover, Polygon utilized multi-chain framework, and periodic checkpoints that bringing additional layer of security. Polygon is PoS based and utilized MATIC token for securing the Polygon network and rewards distribution. As result, Polygon provides high throughput and less Gas fees and high compatibility with Ethereum smart contracts.

The details of the Proposed System architecture and proposed framework is discussed in detail in Chapter 4.

3.4. Selection of technologies, Tools and frameworks for Blockchain based Architecture

In proposed system design, various tools and technology were used apart from blockchain to support blockchain based Architecture are defined in this section.

3.4.1. Decentralized Storage Solution - Inter Planetary File System (IPFS)

The proposed solution follows collaborative approach to mitigate volumetric DDoS attacks by employing Blockchain based infrastructure. As part of attacks mitigation process, attacks information files generated after attacks detection required storage that stored attacks information files generated from all collaborators. There are many storage solutions available in market, so carefully evaluation of all storage solutions and selection was required. In storage solutions, traditional centralized storage server, cloud storage and decentralized storage solutions were prominent options. Traditional centralized storage servers come with challenges such as difficult to horizontally scalable and single point of failure. Additionally, to design distributed system, traditional centralized servers are preferred.

Cloud storage provides high scalability and fault tolerance and suitable for distributed system. But Cloud storage follows Centralized server-based storage model and controlled by third-party provider (Cloud vendor such as Amazon, Azure, GCP). Additionally, storage over cloud involves cost as per storage space and bandwidth. Moreover, data privacy and security are biggest concern while designing a collaborative solution, where all participating peers' agreements and consensus required. By considering all these factors, we chosen decentralized storage solutions.

In proposed system design, we utilized IPFS as storage solution for storing attacks signature files in decentralized space. IPFS (Benet, 2014) is a decentralized, Peer to Peer storage solution, follows content based addressing for data integrity and censorship resistance. It provides high scalability and high fault tolerance by distributing stored content across multiple nodes with significant trade-offs in availability, Integrity and data access speed. Additionally, IPFS is designed especially for supporting applications, which are backed by blockchain technology, censorship-resistant publishing, required decentralized storage, and ownership-centric applications. Moreover, IPFS does not charge any subscription fees or storage fees, which is one another factor of consideration. With less or no storage cost, IPFS provides high security, integrity with decentralized application integration support. The proposed solution employed blockchain based infrastructure and followed collaborative approach, IPFS, a decentralized storage was suitable and appropriate choice as a storage solution. In proposed system, attacks signature files securely stored over IPFS and IPFS hashes were stored over Polygon blockchain for accessibility, logging and monitoring. Storing attack signature files over IPFS significantly reduced smart contracts storage (on-chain storage) that directly resulting reduction in Gas consumption. Overall, optimization of on-chain storage and gas consumption are achieved through decentralized storage solution, IPFS in proposed system.

3.4.2. Smart Contracts Development and Deployment language and tools

Smart Contract development Language - In proposed system, Smart contracts are inevitable part of blockchain-based framework for attack information sharing among collaborators. Ethereum-compatible smart contracts which basically write by following Ethereum Virtual Machine (EVM) standards, are compatible with both Ethereum and Polygon blockchains. In proposed system, Smart contracts are written by using Solidity (soliditylang, n.d.) language. Solidity is a statistically typed, high level, Turing-complete programming language used for smart contracts and Token contracts development.

Smart Contract Development and deployment framework or suite - Smart Contracts development and deployment Truffle framework (Truffle Documentation - Truffle Suite, n.d.) was used in proposed framework. Truffle is a most comprehensive suite of tools for smart contracts development. It provides tools for Smart contracts development, debugging, testing and deployment in one suite, with security at first place in whole process and robust Layer 1 and Layer 2 blockchain support. In proposed system, Truffle framework handled Smart contracts development, its compilation and deployment of these compiled smart contracts on Polygon's TestNet named Mumbai TestNet.

Smart Contract deployment TestNet - In proposed system, smart contracts were deployed on Polygon's official TestNet named Mumbai TestNet. In Blockchain Ecosystem, TestNet replicates behavior of Mainnet (main official blockchain), but designed especially for testing Smart contracts and DApps without spending actual crypto tokens, mainly used for validating and checking behavior of smart contracts before deploying them to actual Mainnet. In this research study, we deployed proposed system's smart contracts on Mumbai TestNet, but these Smart Contracts were tested meticulous by considering all the security and network requirements of Polygon's Mainnet. So Proposed system's smart contracts are also compatible with Polygon as well as Ethereum Mainnet without modifying smart contracts code. Secondly, Mainnet are mainly optimized as it constantly monitored by validators that improves overall smart contracts and system performance. Whereas TestNet faces some problems related to Network latency and node availability that slightly impact Smart contracts performance. Lastly, all other related research studies deployed their smart contracts on respective TestNets, this was one of the reasons for opting TestNet over Mainnet for comparative perspective.

3.5. Data Generation and Input (Attacks traffic generation)

In Proposed system, Blockchain based architecture was used for volumetric DDoS attacks mitigation collaboratively. In proposed system data was generated by simulating various volumetric DDoS attacks on controlled testbed environment and on real network. The proposed Blockchain based collaborative solution was implemented and deployed in real time. But proposed mitigation solution was tested by simulating volumetric DDoS attacks through various network traffic generation tools. There are several reasons why we simulate volumetric DDoS attacks for validating proposed solution. Firstly, the proposed solution falls under experimental research, applied research, and mitigate volumetric DDoS attacks collaboratively by leveraging blockchain based architecture. This proposed system tried to solve real time collaboration problem to protect group of participating organizations(collaborators) from volume-based DDoS attacks through collaborative mitigation approach. So, evaluation of the proposed system, we generated our own simulation traffic by considering various standard datasets of DDoS attacks traffic data such as CICIDS2017, NSL-KDD, CICIDS2017, and CICDoS2016 etc. Secondly, it is not feasible and hard to access real world DDoS attacks traffic data or real time network logs while actual DDoS attacks due to privacy and security standards. So, for proposed system testing and validation simulation of volumetric DDoS attacks was only feasible option. By considering all these reasons, we simulated and emulated volumetric DDoS attacks to test the proposed solution in controlled testbed environment and real time environment.

Volumetric DDoS attacks data generation (Simulation) - Network traffic data or logs were generated after meticulously considering all standard datasets of traffic logs of DDoS attacks named CICIDS2017, NSL-KDD, CICIDS2017, and CICDoS2016 etc. In Volumetric DDoS attacks, we considered three flooding attacks named ICMP flood, UDP flood and TCP flood against our targeted networks. For network traffic generation we used tool named Hping3 (Kali.org, n.d.) that generated volumetric attack traffic in simulation and real time scenario. Hping3 is a command-line network traffic generation tool especially designed for network testing and performance measurement. Hping3 used for generating attack traffic (TCP, UDP and ICMP traffic) against targeted networks. For normal traffic generation, Scapy (S et al., 2018 & Scapy, n.d.) library was utilized. Scapy is a powerful python-based library for interactive packet manipulation, mainly used for simulating network traffic, Sniffing, simulation of DDoS / DoS attacks, and Penetration testing. For generating UDP and TCP flood attacks traffic (simulation), we also utilized Scapy (Python scripts for generate attacks traffic).

Data related to Proposed Mitigation Solution - The proposed blockchain based mitigation solution included Polygon blockchain data and logs (transactions hash) as attacks information and signatures files stored on IPFS. When attacks detected, attacks signatures files stored over IPFS and its hashes and logs were stored on Polygon blockchain. These IPFS Hashes and transactions hashes and logs permanently exist on Polygon blockchain (Mumbai TestNet). These records are immutable and secured because of backed by blockchain so it could be utilized for monitoring and logging purposes.

The Architecture of the proposed solution and it's the proposed framework are discussed in the next chapter 4.

CHAPTER 4: THE PROPOSED VOLUMETRIC DDOS ATTACKS MITIGATION SOLUTION

This chapter defines Architecture of proposed System and proposed Volumetric DDoS Mitigation framework. This proposed framework mainly intended to solve collaboration problem among participating peers by employing blockchain based architecture, especially in Collaborative DDoS attacks mitigation. In this chapter, we first present Proposed System Architecture. Afterwards, Proposed framework is defined and discusses. This proposed mitigation solution's two categories are also briefly represented. Overall, this chapter is dedicated to the proposed solution design and framework.

4.1. Need of the Proposed Volumetric DDoS attacks Mitigation Solution

This proposed solution aimed to mitigate volumetric DDoS attacks collaboratively by implementing collaborative blockchain based architecture. The traditional DDoS mitigation solutions have many limitations such as mainly centralized in nature, so lack efficient to mitigate DDoS attacks where attacks coordinated distributedly. Secondly, centralized mitigation solution leads to single point of failure and security breaches problems. Lastly, lack of security, privacy and transparency of data are maintained when traditional / centralized mitigation solution implemented because organization's network (victim) traffic managed or filtered through these third-party traditional security vendors. Contrary, when cloud-based mitigation solution deals with attacks distributedly but cloud solutions are not reliable and secured while dealing with highly secured data and sometime data compliance requirements also restricted cloud solutions for attacks mitigation. As cloud-based solutions, directly or indirectly handle organization's traffic for the purpose of scrubbing, filtering or cleaning attack traffic from normal traffic.

These days majority of applications employ distributed architecture because of scalability and efficiency and fault-tolerance nature of distributed architecture. In modern era, it is highly recommendable to design a mitigation solution that follows distributed architecture along with maintained data privacy and confidentiality.

This proposed architecture is designed to address and overcome limitations of tradition / centralized mitigation solutions and fulfills research objective of building collaborative volumetric DDoS mitigation solution that efficiently mitigate attack while concerning data privacy and confidentiality, integrity. Distributed and collaborated attacks mitigation is architected by employing Blockchain based architecture. Additionally, this proposed blockchain based architecture helps to maintain data integrity, security and privacy of attacks signature information which shared by collaborators (participating peers) as part of collaborative DDoS mitigation. Furthermore, because of this proposed blockchain based collaborative architecture, task of repeatedly attack detection at other collaborators' end is avoided. Whereas attack traffic filtering and detection task handled by individual collaborators, so that individual organizations (collaborators) are independent to handle their own data privacy, integrity and security requirements. This proposed architectural design enables systematic attacks detection, filtering at individual collaborators end, distributed attacks mitigation through blockchain based collaborative approach along with immutable, secured, verifiable event-logging and monitoring - directly align with the proposed system objectives of efficient volumetric DDoS attacks mitigation in collaborative environment.

4.2. Architecture of Proposed Volumetric DDoS attacks Mitigation Solution

In this section, we discussed overall system architecture of proposed solution. First, major components of proposed system architected are described in detail.

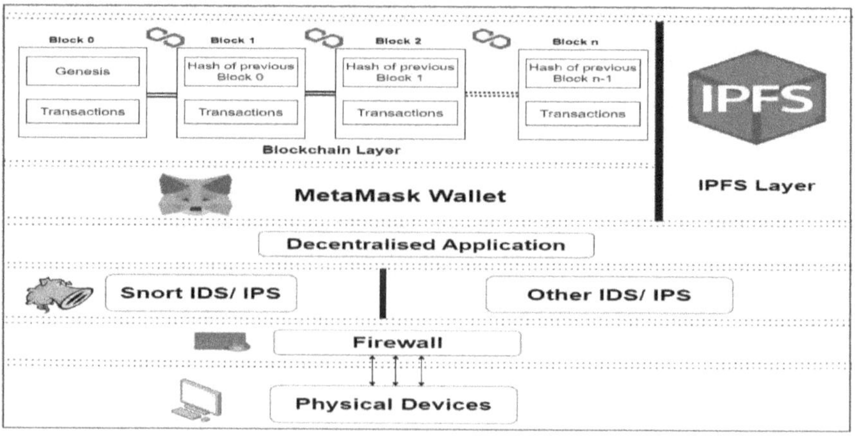

Figure 4.1 Proposed System Architecture

Blockchain Layer – This Blockchain layer is prominent in proposed system architecture. In proposed system design, we selected Polygon blockchain to build collaboration process open, transparent and secured among collaborators (participating peers or networks). This blockchain layer aimed to act as collaborative medium through that the collaborators shared attacks signatures and attacks information among other collaborators for efficient attack detection and mitigation at other collaborators' end. Based on these attacks signature efficient attacks detection and mitigation strategies pre-implemented at other collaborators' end, that basically reveals prevention and mitigation aspect of proposed system.

Interaction to this blockchain layer has happened through Ethereum based smart contracts deployed over Polygon's blockchain. In this proposed system, we deployed three Ethereum based smart contracts over Mumbai's TestNet. Smart contracts invocation becomes input of this layer. MetaMask (Metamask, n.d.) and proposed system's DApps generally invoked these smart contracts smart contracts. This blockchain layer communicates with IPFS Layer to store attacks information files over IPFS, and as result, attack signature files' hash retrieved from the IPFS to blockchain layer. Smart contracts interactions and logs registered on-chain as result of these transactions, which could be utilized for monitoring and logging purposes.

IPFS Layer / Attacks Data Storage Layer – The IPFS Layer also referred as Attacks data storage layer responsible for storing and retrieving attacks signature files data in decentralized manner. In proposed architecture, IPFS provides high degree of decentralized storage of data, and support decentralized blockchain based infrastructure as IPFS and blockchain share high level of integration. IPFS securely stored attacks information files shared by collaborators in secured, transparent manner and provides faster data retrieval upon request. IPFS layer communicates with Blockchain layer through smart contracts, attacks signature file becomes input to IPFS layer. Afterwards, IPFS provides stored file hash in response. Through this stored file hash, other collaborators can access this stored attack signature file with the help of smart contracts.

MetaMask Wallet – The MetaMask wallet (Metamask, n.d.) plays proviral role to connect proposed system's DApps with Blockchain layer. MetaMask is a crypto-currency wallet and supports Decentralized Applications or DApps. MetaMask plays Account manager role when registering a new collaborator (a participating network or peer) in proposed system. Additionally, user authentication, transaction signing and network management tasks are also handled through MetaMask in proposed DApps. In proposed system, MetaMask is a prerequisite to connect with proposed DApps. Based on DApps interactions appropriate actions are taken placed on Mumbai TestNet thanks to this abstraction layer of MetaMask. And MetaMask also handles DApps rendering and changes according to the blockchain state changes. In this proposed solution, we used MetaMask browser extension to connect with MetaMask wallet.

Decentralized Application (DApps) - The proposed DApps serves as a medium between Blockchain based infrastructure and attack detection, prevention system of individual collaborator's Network. Decentralized Applications is a web-based application that runs on top of blockchain, and responsible for providing user interaction with blockchain. In general, DApps contains web-based frontend (mobile interface) for user interaction and smart contracts for blockchain integration in backend side. Data of Volumetric DDoS attacks detected (Attacks signature files) by Attack detection layer becomes input to this DApps. This Proposed DApps considers as a platform where attacks signature files are shared by collaborators upon detection of attacks. In proposed DApps, front-end is built using Javascript library React.js and backend integrated various Ethereum based Smart contracts run on top of Polygon blockchain, IPFS through Web3 library.

Attack Detection Layer – The Attack Detection layer responsible for volumetric DDoS attacks detection at individual collaborators' network. This attack detection layer basically resides at network gateway of collaborators' Network. So, network's inbound and outbound traffic become input to this detection layer. In this proposed architecture, the attack detection layer analyzed network's inbound traffic and based on IDS, IPS rulesets, attack signature file is going to get created by this layer. Afterwards, this attacks signature file inputted to blockchain based infrastructure through proposed DApps. In this proposed Architecture, we utilized Snort (Snort, 2023), an open-source Network IDS and IPS software for attacks detection at individual collaborators' end. Snort generally utilized for network traffic analysis and packet inspection for detection and prevention of network attacks in real time. As attacks detection is beyond the scope of proposed system, we designed the proposed system architecture by considering flexibility of selecting appropriate attack detection and prevention system at individual collaborators' end. But for evaluating the proposed solution, we employed Snort for IDS and IPS as it provides custom rules creation and cross-platform compatibility so majority of collaborators could run snort without changing their existing security infrastructure.

Attack Mitigation Layer – This Attack mitigation layer serves as last layer in proposed infrastructure. This attack Mitigation layer responsible for attack mitigation through blocking source of volumetric attacks. After attack detection at individual collaborators' end, or part of attack prevention measures (attack signature files), Snort provides list of blacklisted IP addresses, that become input to Attack Mitigation Layer. Afterwards, this Attack Mitigation Layer is blocked malicious IP addresses. So rather than blocking specific packets this attack source blocking approach is more efficient in volume-based DDoS attacks mitigation. In this proposed architecture, we took An IP blocking Firewall, that is a host-based firewall, software firewall for evaluating proposed solution. We designed this proposed architecture with flexibility in terms of selection of appropriate IP blocking firewall at individual collaborators' end.

4.2.1. Inter-Module Communication and Data Flow

In this section, we defined how different system components and layers within the proposed system interact with each other and data flow among different components and layers. It provides clear view of how data or information is transferred, processed throughout the proposed system. The proposed system inter-module communication starts when volumetric DDoS attacks detected through snort, and it generates attacks signature files. But before this communication begins there are some prerequisites, registration process of network or peer (collaborator) in proposed system through following some steps. Afterwards, normal data flow of attacks mitigation happened in proposed system.

Register a network as a collaborator in Proposed system, and network configuration for Volumetric DDoS attacks mitigation at individual collaborator's end, the detailed data flow is given in below.

- A proposed collaborator (a network or a peer) first time navigates to the proposed system DApps, they need to complete registration to MetaMask wallet if they are a new user of MetaMask. Or if they are existing customer of MetaMask, then simply signing to their MetaMask wallet.
- A proposed collaborator to connect their MetaMask wallet to the Proposed DApps by following instructions given on the Proposed DApps. In this step, authentication process follows strictly by utilizing MetaMask.

- Afterwards, by following instructions over the proposed DApps, connect their MetaMask wallet to Mumbai TestNet of Polygon for invoking smart contracts.
- After collaborator registration, individual network gets detailed instructions to integrate Attacks detection Layer (especially Snort) for attacks detection (default option), or otherwise collaborators are independent to choose other Attacks detection, prevention system. For that integrate these custom selected IPS, IDS with blockchain based infrastructure for collaborative attacks mitigation. In the proposed DApps all these integration instructions are given.
- For Attack mitigation and blocking IP blocking Firewall is employed by default. The detailed instruction is given for how to integrate Attack detection layer with Attack mitigation layer at individual collaborator's end.

As result of these collaborator registration process, a network that intended to mitigate volumetric DDoS attacks, register on the proposed system collaboration and get involved in attacks detection, mitigation and prevention process transparently and securely.

The Data flow of proposed system to mitigate volumetric DDoS attacks are as follows:

- At every collaborator's end, Attack detection layer continuously observes and analyzes (sniff) network's inbound traffic based on Snort rulesets, (attack detections system rulesets) and detects volumetric DDoS attacks.
- When attacks detected at Victim collaborator's end, Attacks Detection layer communicate with Attack Mitigation Layer, and provides malicious IP addresses to Attack Mitigation Layer for attack source blocking through Snort integration to IP blocking firewall. As result, attack is going to blocked at victim collaborator's end.
- After Attacks detection at Victim collaborator's end, Snort generates attacks signature file contains malicious IP addresses through which volumetric DDoS attacks originated.

- This attack information file is going to get uploaded to the proposed DApps by Victim collaborator through invocation of Smart contract by signing transaction through MetaMask.
- This invoked smart contract, that first uploads the attack signature file to IPFS.
- IPFS receives files as input and provide unique IPFS file hash (upon file upload) in response to this invoked Smart contract.
- This invoked Smart contract stores this IPFS file hash over Polygon blockchain by changing state of the blockchain.
- MetaMask sings all the transactions of invoked smart contracts and send it to Polygon blockchain in whole interaction of blockchain layer.
- At other collaborators' end, Attack Detection Layer (Snort) constantly communicate to DApps for attacks signature information.
- When Victim collaborator uploads attack signature file, all other collaborators' Attack Detection layer (Snort) retrieves attack information file from the proposed DApps.
- Other collaborators read the IPFS hash of attack signature file from Polygon blockchain.
- And retrieved Attack signature file from IPFS through the proposed DApps.
- This attack information file is shared to Attack Detection Layer (Snort) of individual Collaborator.
- Attack Detection Layer creates new rules for blacklisting the traffic originated from IP addresses mentioned in the Attack signature File.
- If any attack traffic detected at Attack detection Layer originated from blacklisted IP addresses, Snort instantly communicates with Attack Mitigation layer.
- Attack Mitigation Layer is going to block malicious IP addresses with the help of Snort integration.

- Attack traffic originated from blacklisted IP addresses automatically blocked without overload of attack traffic inspection at other collaborators' end.

4.2.2. Data Security consideration in Proposed System

In whole inter-module data communication, security of data is highly considered. At Attack Detection and Mitigation layer, data security rules are integrated in Snort and Firewall. Next, At the proposed DApps security is implemented through integration of MetaMask and authentication mechanism, to prevent authorized data access. In the proposed DApps level, only blockchain hashes are stored and accessible only to verified collaborator, and these hashes are cryptographically secured especially in Polygon blockchain, Keccak-256 (SHA – 3 variant) is used for hashing. At MetaMask Layer, Data security is enforced through transaction signing and encryption, provided by MetaMask Wallet. All the accounts at MetaMask strictly authenticated backed by seed phase to prevent unauthenticated access. Subsequently, security at IPFS layer is enforced through its built-in features such as immutability (once file uploaded, it cannot be changed), CID (Content identifier – each file recognized by this hash). IPFS internally stored file content by breaking file into multiple chunks and generates hash of each chunk, finally CID is created so whole file is not stored at one location, but encrypted and hashed file chunks are stored distributed over multiple location, which provides high security to file data.

Lastly, Hash of IPFS file is stored over Polygon blockchain, which is backed by inherited security of Polygon blockchain that provides immutability, encryption of transaction data, security to the IPFS file hashes data. Additionally, Smart contracts are created by considering security requirements, and smart contracts audits already performed to meet Smart contracts security standards. By evaluating security consideration of each layer, and its interactions, the proposed framework met data security requirements of architectural design.

4.3. Proposed Volumetric DDoS attacks Mitigation Framework

In this section, we defined a framework of proposed solution to mitigate volumetric DDoS attacks. The proposed framework consists of two main modules that integrates and works combinedly to mitigate volumetric DDoS attacks. These two modules are Intra-network Volumetric DDoS Mitigation Scheme and Collaborative volumetric DDoS Mitigation Scheme.

4.3.1. Intra-network Volumetric DDoS Mitigation Scheme

Intra-network volumetric DDoS mitigation scheme contains various components such as Attacks Detection Layer, Attacks Mitigation Layer of proposed system architecture to mitigate volumetric DDoS attacks at individual collaborators' end. This Intra-network scheme aims to implement attacks detection, and mitigation internally at individual collaborators' end where collaborator is independent to choose their own mitigation and detection tools according to their own network policy. Figure 4.2 shows Intra-network Volumetric DDoS Mitigation Scheme.

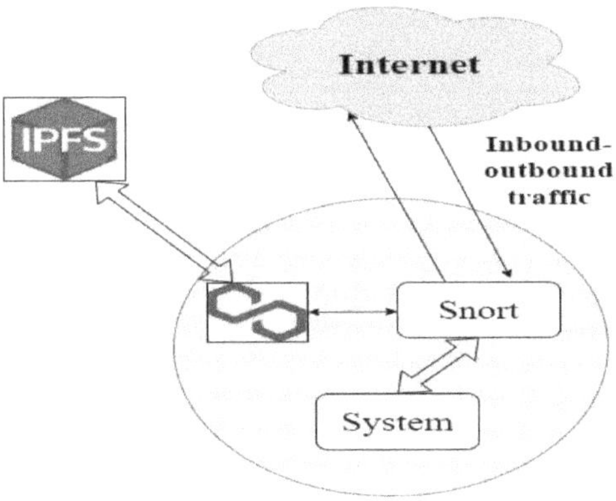

Figure 4.2 Intra-network Volumetric DDoS Mitigation Scheme of Proposed Framework

For proposed system, we utilized Snort for attacks detection and employed an IP blocking Firewall for Attack Mitigation layer by default. This Attack detection Layer basically placed at internet gateway that directly evaluates and inspects inwards and outwards traffic to and from internet gateway. Additionally, this Attack Detection Layer

(Snort) directly connected to Attack Mitigation Layer (An IP blocking Firewall). Snort (or other IDS / IPS) generates an alert when unwanted traffic patterns or behavior are detected. Afterwards, malicious IP addresses detected at Attack Detection Layer, shared to Attacks Mitigation Layer for attacks mitigation. At Attack Mitigation layer, these malicious IP addresses are blocked through Firewall to stop receiving traffic from source of attacks. Subsequently, when Attack Detection Layer generates alert for possible volumetric DDoS attacks, Attack detection layer (Snort) generates an attack signature file that contains Illegitimates IP addresses (attack source IP addresses detected by Snort or other IDS / IPS) and network traces files for monitoring and logging purpose. These files would be utilized by Collaborative Volumetric DDoS Mitigation Scheme for collaborative attacks mitigation.

Moreover, In Intra-network scheme, Attack Detection Layer connected to the Proposed system's Decentralized Application (DApps) to become part of Collaborative Volumetric DDoS Mitigation Scheme of the proposed solution.

4.3.2 Collaborative Volumetric DDoS Mitigation Scheme

This Collaborative Volumetric DDoS Mitigation Scheme aims to mitigate volumetric DDoS attacks collaboratively by combining capabilities of all collaborators in secured and transparent manner. This Collaborative Volumetric DDoS Mitigation Scheme contains different components such as DApps, MetaMask wallet, Blockchain Layer and IPFS layer especially blockchain based architecture. This proposed scheme mainly facilitates open, transparent and secured collaboration among all collaborators and mitigates volumetric DDoS attacks collaboratively.

In Collaborative Volumetric DDoS Mitigation Scheme, all collaborators (participating networks or Peers) share the same interest in attack detection, mitigation, and defense to contribute to volumetric DDoS attacks mitigation. As shown in Figure 4.3 each of the collaborators is connected to the Polygon's Mumbai TestNet (Blockchain Layer) through the MetaMask wallet by our Decentralized Application (Dapp). And blockchain layer directly connected to IPFS layer to store attacks signature files. Every collaborator that participated in collaboration and contributed to volumetric DDoS attacks mitigation by implementing the Intra-network volumetric DDoS mitigation scheme at their own network level. Afterwards, each of the collaborators registers their network as a collaborator by invoking addCollaborator smart contracts in the proposed

Decentralized Application (DApps). Invocation of the addCollaborator smart contracts is prerequisite for register a collaborator in Collaborative Volumetric DDoS Mitigation Scheme.

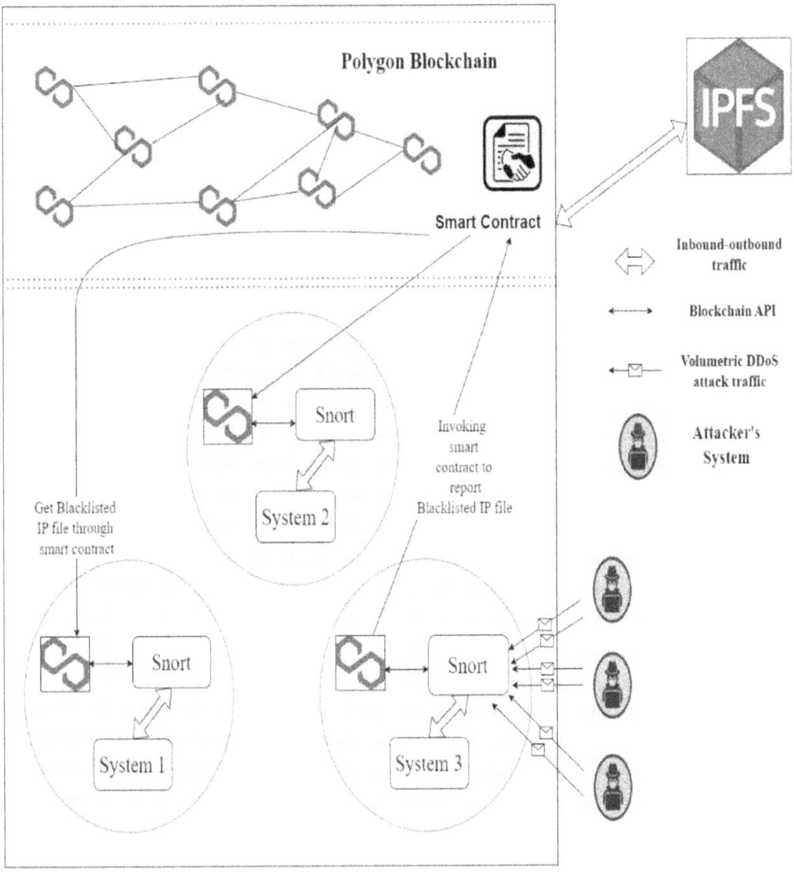

Figure 4.2 Collaborative Volumetric DDoS Mitigation Scheme of Proposed Framework

After registered as a collaborator, a collaborator can report attacks signature or attack logs files by invoking the ipfsHashStorage smart contract through the proposed DApps (after reporting attacks information a collaborator called a reporter collaborator). This ipfsHashStorage smart contract is collaborator-wise individual and single, means individual collaborator becomes owner of the pfsHashStorage smart contract. And individual collaborator deployed this smart contract only once when they first report the attack signature file, then after all the reporting file hashes are stored in the same contract, we proposed this design because of smart contract's limited storage capability, auditability and high Gas fees and traceability. If we had directly stored attack information on smart contracts, it would have consumed more Gas and storage because of all attack data storage over on-chain. Storage and Gas consumptions are significant factors while utilization of smart contracts for DDoS attacks mitigation. Optimization of on-chain storage and Gas consumption drastically improves system performance and implementation costs. This ipfsHashStorage smart contract internally stored file to IPFS and IPFS Hash of the attack's information file writes on the same (own) contract. For attacks signature file storage, we utilized IPFS, which provide high security, scalability, efficiency, traceability to the proposed system.

After reporting the attack signature files which contains Blacklisted IP address of volumetric DDoS attacks detected by Reporter collaborator, other receiver collaborators (networks) get this file through the proposed DApps and utilized it as input to their Attack Detection Layer (Snort / other IDS). As a result, other collaborators would mitigate and prevent possible volumetric DDoS attacks through their Intra-network Volumetric DDoS Mitigation Scheme. Due to this Collaborative Volumetric DDoS Mitigation Scheme attack prevention measures are taken in advanced and repeated attacks detection and mitigation overhead on another collaborator's end going to get avoided.

4.3.2.1 Proposed Decentralized Application (DApps) - POLY-DDOSCHAIN

The proposed system DApps named POLY-DDOSCHAIN is a central component for all collaborators who wants to participate in Collaborative Volumetric DDoS Mitigation Scheme for the purposed of collaborative volumetric DDoS attacks mitigation in transparent, secured and decentralized manner. The POLY-DDOSCHAIN DApps is a medium that connects collaborators to the Polygon blockchain (Mumbai TestNet as proposed solution deployed on it) and IPFS through the POLY-DDOSCHAIN smart contracts.

The main intention behind designing this proposed Dapp is to make the collaboration process transparent, secured and distributed through enforcing strong authentication to restrict unauthorized access to the Polygon blockchain for collaboration purpose. This POLY-DDOSCHAIN DApp is connected to the Polygon blockchain (Mumbai TestNet) through the MetaMask wallet (APIs). This proposed DApp becomes an interface to invoke the POLY-DDOSCHAIN smart contracts deployed on the Mumbai TestNet, connect to IPFS and other blockchain based infrastructure. We launched this POLY-DDOSCHAIN DApps over internet and its backend runs on top of blockchain based infrastructure. The web-based application (mobile interface) operates over internet, provides user interface responsible for user interaction and collaboration. Whereas backend is responsible for connection over polygon blockchain and IPFS. In proposed DApps, front-end is built using Javascript library React.js and backend integrated various Ethereum based Smart contracts run on top of Polygon blockchain, IPFS through Web3 library.

4.3.2.2 POLY-DDOSCHAIN Smart Contracts

This section is adapted from ours's previously published work (Patel, Darshi, 2024). It outlines the POLY-DDOSCHAIN Smart Contracts introduction, its initialization and its design.

In the proposed solution, POLY-DDOSCHAIN Smart Contracts play significant role in building open, transparent and decentralized collaboration among collaborators come from untrusted environment by providing a medium of interaction to Polygon blockchain. In this section, POLY-DDOSCHAIN Smart contracts initialization and Smart contracts design are briefly discussed.

We consider that the collaboration process between different participant networks(collaborators) would be managed by an administrative organization (Contract Owner) transparently and securely. We use blockchain that brings transparency, security, authenticity, and immutability to collaboration between heterogeneous networks aimed at collaborative volumetric DDoS attacks mitigation. Here, we use the Polygon blockchain to run smart contracts. We developed our smart contracts in Solidity that brings Smart contracts flexibility so that Smart contracts can run on multiple platforms such as Ethereum and Polygon.

In the proposed solution, we created three smart contracts: 1). addCollaborator smart contract, 2). addAllHashStorage smart contract, 3). addIpfsHashStorage smart contract. Here, the Administrative organization deployed the addCollaborator smart contract and addAllHashStorage smart contract. Whereas addIpfsHashStorage smart contract is deployed by a collaborator when a collaborator reports an attack signature and suspicious IP addresses.

The addCollaborator smart contract includes collaborators' addresses and is deployed by the administrative organization to store all the addresses of the collaborator's nodes. The smart contract allows Individual networks and systems to register themselves as a collaborator, check collaborator status, retrieve other collaborators' addresses of the proposed collaboration, and the total count of all collaborators participating in the POLY-DDOSCHAIN (proposed) collaboration.

Another smart contract named addAllHashStorage aimed to store the mapping of a collaborator and addIpfsHashStorage smart contract hash value deployed by a collaborator. It includes senderHash value (collaborator address) and contractHash value (addIpfsHashStorage hash). The administrative organization deploys this contract after the collaborator registration process is completed, and a collaborator wants to report the attack information. A collaborator can register their deployed addIpfsHashStorage hash value, retrieve stored records, and get record counts functions provided by the addAllHashStorage contract.

The addIpfsHashStorage smart contract is developed to store the hash generated by uploading suspicious IP addresses and attack signature files on IPFS. Collaborator-wise, only one addIpfsHashStorage smart contract is deployed at a time when a collaborator reports a file of suspicious IP addresses and attack signatures for the first time. It includes the ipfsHash value and the contract owner's address. The smart contract allows adding the IpfsHash value, retrieving the IpfsHash value, checking the IpfsHash value, and counting the number of IpfsHash values. Only the owner of this smart contract can access and call these functions of the addIpfsHashStorage smart contract.

POLY-DDOSCHAIN Smart Contracts Desing

Smart Contracts of POLY-DDOSCHAIN are developed using the Solidity language, a high-level, statically typed, and Turing-complete programming language used to write smart contracts and token contracts. Two types of accounts in Polygon Blockchain. First, externally owned accounts (EOA) are used to send transactions to other EOA then after initiate and invoke transactions to deploy a smart contract on the Polygon blockchain (Mumbai TestNet). Public and private keys are associated with the EOAs. In contrast, a contract account (CA) is an account that stores and runs the code of the smart contract. A contract account is created by deploying a smart contract through an EOA. Contract accounts do not own any public or private keys. There are three smart contracts in the proposed solution. So first, we describe smart contract initialization (defines state variables of the contract) and the functions of every POLY-DDOSCHAIN's Smart Contracts.

(i) addCollaborator Smart contract Initialization:

- storedAddresses: stores addresses of the collaborators. It is an array of the addresses (collaborator' addresses). Aimed to easily find out collaborator's address and cost effective.

The addCollaborator contract mainly provides the following functionals where a collaborator is denoted as C.

*checkCollaborator(*C.EOA(*maddress))*: this function checks whether the given address is collaborator or not, it returns true is C.EOA(maddress) is exist in the addCollaborator contract, otherwise it returns false. It would be invoked at time to register a new collaborator (Algorithm 2) and allow other functionality based on the result of this function. The logic of this function is demonstrated in Algorithm 1.

addAddress(C.EOA(newAddress)) : algorithm 2 illustrates the logic of this function. It takes input as a new Externally Owned Account Address and adds this new address to the storedAddresses array. It would be called when a new collaborator wants to register in the system.

Algorithm 1. checkCollaborator

```
Algorithm 1. checkCollaborator

Input: C.EOA (maddress)

Output: bool

Convert maddress to bytes20 (bytesAddress1)

For each address in storedAddresses:

        Convert the address in storedAddresses to bytes20 (bytesAddress2)

        If bytesAddress1 is equal to bytesAddress2 then

            Return true;

End

End

If no match is found

        Return false;

End

End
```

Algorithm 2. addAddress

```
Algorithm 2. addAddress

Input: C.EOA (newaddress)

Output: null

If checkCollaborator(newaddress) is equal to false then

    Stored Addresses.push(c.EOA(newadddress))

    emit Collaborator Added(c.EOA(newadddress))

End

Else

    Revert with an error message: "A Collaborator is already registered."

End

End
```

(ii) addAllHashStorage Smart contract Initialization:

- hashDataArray: is an array of structure named hashData which have two elements: senderHash, contractHash of type address. Here senderHash is a collaborator hash and contractHash is a hash of contract deployed by respective collaborator.

The addAllHashStorage contract mainly provides the following functionals where a collaborator is denoted as C.

setHash(C.EOA(senderHash), contractHash): stores the mapping of collaborator hash value(senderHash) and his deployed addIpfsHashStorage contract hash value(contractHash) to the hashDataArray an array of structure named (HashData). It would be called at a time when a collaborator deploys the addIpfsHashStorage smart contract. The logic of this function is presented in Algorithm 3.

getContractHashFromSender(C.EOA(senderHash)) : Algorithm 4 illustrates logic of this function. Aimed to provide deployed contractHash value (deployed addIpfsHashStorage contract) by passing a collaborator hash value(senderHash). Mainly called this function when to interact with the functions of the addIpfsHashStorage contracts.

Algorithm 3. setHash

Algorithm 3. setHash

Input: C.EOA (senderHash), contractHash

Output: null

```
hashDataArray.push(hashData(c.EOA(senderHash), contractHash))
        emit AllHashDataAdded(c.EOA(senderHash), contractHash)
End
```

Algorithm 4. getContractHashFromSender

```
Algorithm 4. getContractHashFromSender
Input: C.EOA (senderHash)
Output: contractHash
For each element in hashDataArray:
  If the senderHash in the current element matches the input senderHash:
      Return the contractHash from the current element
  End
End
If no match is found:
  Revert with an error message: "Sender hash not found"
End
End
```

(iii)addIpfsHashStorage smart contract Initialization:

- contractOwner: stores the hash value of a collaborator who deploy this contract.
- ipfsHash: it is a string type variable which stores IPFS hash value which would be retrieved because of uploading suspicious IP addresses file and attack data on IPFS.

The addIpfsHashStorage contract mainly provides the following functionals where a IpfsHash is denoted as H.

checkIPFSHash(mstring) : this function checks whether the given mstring(hash value) already exists in the contract or not. ipfsHash is an array which stores the IPFS hash values generated because of suspicious IP addresses files or attack signatures files uploaded on the IPFS. This function is only invoked by the contract owner means a respective collaborator who deploys the addIpfsHashStorage contract. Algorithm 5 depicts the logic of this function.

addIPFSHash(newIPFSHash) : only contract owners can call this function otherwise error occurs. Aimed to add newIPFSHash value to the ipfsHash array when checkIPFSHash(mstring) returns false otherwise it returns with error message. The Logic of the function is illustrated in Algorithm 6.

Algorithm 5. checkIPFSHash

```
Algorithm 5. checkIPFSHash
Input: H (mstring)
Output: bool
If message.sender is owner then
  For each element in ipfsHash:
      Calculate the keccak256 hash of the current element and store it as hash1
      Calculate the keccak256 hash of H(mstring) and store it as hash2
      If hash1 is equal to hash2:
            Return true
End
  End
  If no match is found:
      Return false
  End
Else
Revert with an error message: "You are not a contract owner"
End
End
```

Algorithm 6. addIPFSHash

```
Algorithm 6. addIPFSHash
Input: H(newIPFSHash)
Output: null
If message.sender is owner then
        If checkIPFSHash(newIPFSHash) is equal to false then
                ipfsHash.push(H(newIPFSHash))
                emit IpfsHashAdded(H(newIPFSHash))
        End
        Else
                Revert with an error message: "The IPFS Hash already added."
        End
End
Else
        Revert with an error message: "You are not a contract owner"
End
End
```

These POLY-DDOSCHAIN Smart Contracts have significant place in the proposed Blockchain based Architecture. These POLY-DDOSCHAIN Smart Contracts are deployed on Polygon blockchain (Mumbai TestNet) and invoked, initiated through the POLY-DDOSCHAIN DApps with the help of Web3 library and APIs (Patel, Darshi, 2024). The POLY-DDOSCHAIN Smart Contracts deployment details and its explanation are provided in Chapter 4.

Summary

The Chapter is dedicated to the Proposed Volumetric DDoS attacks Mitigation Solution. In starting of this Chapter, we briefly discussed about Need of the proposed solution. Then after, the proposed solution's Architecture is defined by describing different system components, its inter-module communication and security consideration of proposed solution. Afterwards, the Proposed Volumetric DDoS attacks Mitigation Framework that contains two schemes Inter-network and Collaborative schemes are demonstrated briefly. In Collaborative Volumetric DDoS Mitigation Scheme, proposed system's DApps named POLY-DDOSCHAIN DApps and Smart Contracts of proposed system, POLY-DDOSCHAIN Smart Contracts are defined in subsequent sub-sections.

CHAPTER 5: IMPLEMENTATION OF THE PROPOSED VOLUMETRIC DDOS ATTACKS MITIGATION SYSTEM

This chapter defines implementation of the proposed Volumetric DDoS Attacks Mitigation Solution and validate this proposed solution through performing volumetric DDoS attacks on Experimental bases and real time network. First, implementation details of Proposed Volumetric DDoS Attacks Mitigation solution are presented. Afterwards, Simulation of Volumetric DDoS attacks details and its implementation details are briefly discussed. Then after, Simulation of Volumetric DDoS attacks on Distributed Network are presented. Finally, the proposed solution is further evaluated on real time, so the subsequent section presented the Emulation / Simulation of Volumetric DDoS attacks on real Network.

5.1. Implementation of Proposed Volumetric DDoS Attacks Mitigation solution

The proposed solution mainly categorized into two categories: Intra-network Volumetric DDoS Mitigation Scheme and Collaborative volumetric DDoS Mitigation Scheme. Both schemes integrated and work together for the purposed of Volumetric DDoS Mitigation. As discussed in previous chapter, Inter-network mitigation scheme intended to detect and mitigate volumetric attacks at an individual collaborator's network (domain) level. Whereas Collaborative mitigation scheme involves all the participated collaborators for attacks detection, prevention and mitigation in decentralized manner. As both schemes are intended to serve different purposes, its implementation details are also varied based upon the scheme. In subsequent sub-sections we discussed implementation of both schemes in details.

5.1.1. Implementation of Intra-network Volumetric DDoS Mitigation Scheme

In this section, the implementation of Intra-network Volumetric DDoS Mitigation Scheme is shown in detail. This Intra-network scheme's main objective is to detect and mitigate volumetric DDoS attacks within individual collaborator's end (network or domain). From implementation perspective, we implemented Snort in Attack Detection Layer at internet gateways of all collaborators for attacks detection purpose. Snort is an open-source IDS / IPS that we employed at network's gateway, so it constantly analyzed inbound and outbound traffic based on predefined rulesets. Additionally, for the analysis purpose, we utilized a network tool named Wireshark ((Wireshark, n.d.) & (*Learn Wireshark*, n.d.)) only for the analysis and evaluation of network trace data after completion of experiment. Wireshark is an open-source Network Packet analyzer, that mainly utilized for network traffic capturing and analyses. It is mainly used for troubleshooting, security analysis, deep package inspection, protocol development, and various network analysis based on network trace data.

At Attack Mitigation Layer, we employed IP blocking Firewall for blocking the source of volumetric DDoS attacks. The Attack Mitigation Layer aimed to mitigate volumetric DDoS attacks by blocking malicious IP addresses shared by the Attack Detection Layer. From the implementation perspective, IP blocking Firewall, a default firewall of a network or system (a host-based firewall, software firewall) implemented for attacks mitigation purpose. After attacks detection through Snort, a snort generated blacklisted IP address files are inputted to this IP Blocking Firewall, through prewritten scripts. This Attack detection layer that employed IP blocking Firewall blocked the detected attacks by blocking source of attacks traffic. So, attacks source blocking is more efficient compared to packet analysis and then packet blocking. These are some common implementation strategies included in Intra-network Volumetric DDoS Mitigation Scheme implementation. For the specific experiment or attacks simulation, we provided some extra implementation details such as network or system configurations etc. in respective sections.

5.1.2. Implementation of Collaborative Volumetric DDoS Mitigation Scheme

The implementation of Collaborative Volumetric DDoS Mitigation Scheme is described in this section. This collaborative mitigation scheme is aimed to mitigate volumetric DDoS attacks collaboratively by implementing blockchain based infrastructure. This scheme intended to provide transparency and security in collaboration process along with collaborative volumetric DDoS mitigation. Mainly four components such as Blockchain layer, IPFS Layer, MetaMask wallet and the proposed system DApps are integrated together to provide collaborative infrastructure to all participating peers (collaborators) for the purpose of collaborative attacks mitigation.

In Collaborative Volumetric DDoS Mitigation Scheme, the proposed DApps – POLY-DDOSCHAIN especially built to provide security, transparency, openness and decentralization on collaboration process. Through this proposed DApps a collaborator can interact with Blockchain and other components. The POLY-DDOSCHAIN becomes an entry point for Smart Contracts invocation that deployed over Polygon blockchain. The proposed DApps includes three Smart contracts that utilized for collaboration purpose and attack information sharing among all participated collaborators. From implementation point of view, we deployed the proposed DApps named POLY-DDOSCHAIN on internet as it provides web-based interface for user-friendly interaction among collaborators. Whereas backend of this DApps runs on Polygon blockchain (Mumbai TestNet), All three Smart contracts are deployed on Mumbai TestNet. Smart Contract deployment details are provided in Table 5.1.

Details of POLY-DDOSCHAIN smart contracts creation transactions in Mumbai Test Network		
1	**addCollaborator Contract**	
	TxHash	0x0dee07f4326d5978425d2df479668ebc26975a9dd790174735101b35942a26cc
	Time-stamp	Aug-19-2023 05:43:35 PM +UTC
	From	0x799c48fd5b29fbb0c5f2a4d46186d51a159d5ec8
	To	0x0a18dbdc515c44b0e3706dd994df6c3fa665f176
	Transaction Fee	0.0007498125047988 MATIC
2	**addAllHashStorage Contract**	
	TxHash	0xe880c9b3b2062753206e405ab1df8a4e9d59933ee75dfe719b921c77533a5f36
	Time-stamp	Aug-19-2023 05:49:53 PM +UTC
	From	0x799c48fd5b29fbb0c5f2a4d46186d51a159d5ec8
	To	0x1a5766e46a0a8f0732e56b97369334c65c19268c

	Transaction Fee	0.001052430006735552 MATIC
3	**addIpfsHashStorage Contract**	
	TxHash	0xe0afce236c954efcc51c3945053cf10a167e3ac47674f6965484befac140bfd7
	Time-stamp	Aug-25-2023 01:05:37 PM +UTC
	From	0xf6a6c6127e6dc60790ce0e9a2956c787b7e7b278
	To	0xaa974a38e22d12fcefc1a202f5ae95cd632ca954
	Transaction Fee	0.000342282502327521 MATIC

[Table 5.1: POLY-DDOSCHAIN Smart Contracts Creation Details]

This paragraph and Table 5.1 are taken from ours's previously published work (Patel, Darshi, 2024). It outlines the POLY-DDOSCHAIN Smart Contracts interaction, attacks mitigation process that combines both schemes and Smart Contract deployment details over Mumbai TestNet. Collaborative Volumetric DDoS Mitigation Scheme 's participation process starts with invoking the addCollaborator smart contract; as a result, the participant network becomes a collaborator in the system. Then, a collaborator deploys his addIpfsHashStoarage smart contract through the proposed DApps. When a victim collaborator detects attacks, snort creates a file of suspicious IP addresses and attack patterns, subsequently, victim collaborator performs actions for attack mitigation by utilizing this attack detection information according to the attack mitigation policy in the victim network. Then, this snort-generated file is uploaded on IPFS through the proposed DApps. The IPFS file hash, that returned in response to the attack information file upload on IPFS, is stored on the addIpfsHashStorage contract, and all other collaborators of the proposed solution get this file through the addAllHashStorage contract. So other collaborators use this reported file as an input to their Intra-network Volumetric DDoS Mitigation Scheme and block the illegitimate IP addresses mentioned on the reported file of a victim collaborator before an attack performed on the other collaborator's network means attack prevention, defense, mitigation strategies, and measures are implemented before facing attack traffic in advance. The Figure 5.1 shows addCollaborator Smart Contract transaction details of deployment on Mumbai TestNet in Mumbai TestNet Explorer.

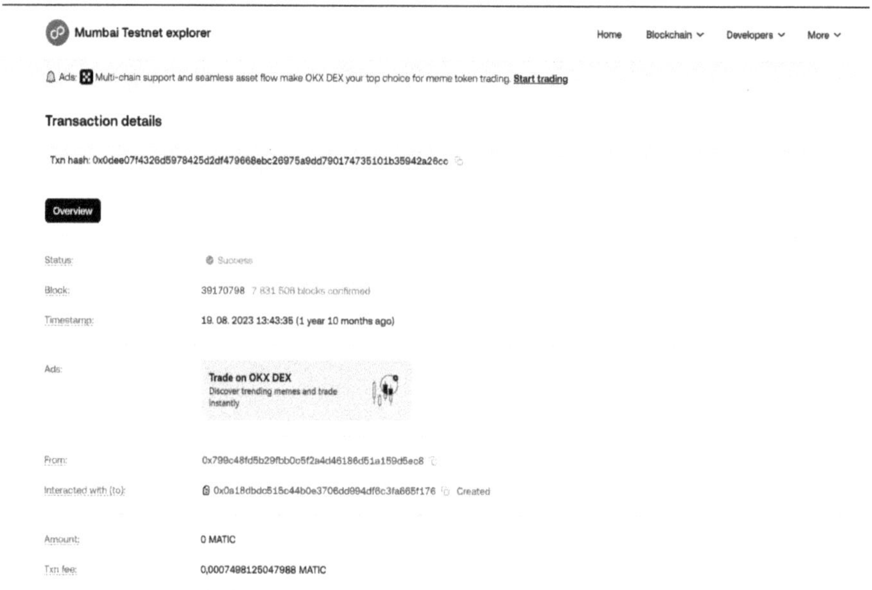

Figure 5.1 addCollaborator Smart Contract transaction details in Mumbai TestNet Explorer

5.2. Simulation of Volumetric DDoS attacks – From implementation point of view

In this proposed system, we simulated volumetric DDoS attacks (UDP flood, TCP flood and ICMP flood) by utilizing real-world attack generation tools and scripts on various network conditions such as (emulation and real-world network scenarios), in order to validate and evaluate the proposed system under volumetric DDoS attacks conditions.

Volumetric DDoS attack simulation was performed through real-world packet and attacks generation tool named hping3 (Kali.org, n.d.). It is a command-line network tool mainly used for purpose of network testing and performance measurement. The hping3 generates custom packets and send these custom packets to Victim network. In the proposed research, the hping3 tool utilized to generate ICMP flood, UDP flood, and TCP flood attacks towards the victim network (Victim collaborator). Additionally, a powerful Python based interactive packet manipulation library named Scapy ((S et al., 2018) & (Scapy, n.d.)) is used to simulate UDP flood and TCP flood attacks. Moreover, for generation of normal regular traffic (Legitimate traffic) this Scapy library is utilized to write normal traffic generation scripts. Additionally, traffic from normal internet surfing activities and internal network traffic, which were also considered and included along with the simulated attacks traffic while performing various experiments. TCP flood attack traffic generation script written in Scapy library shown in Figure 5.2.

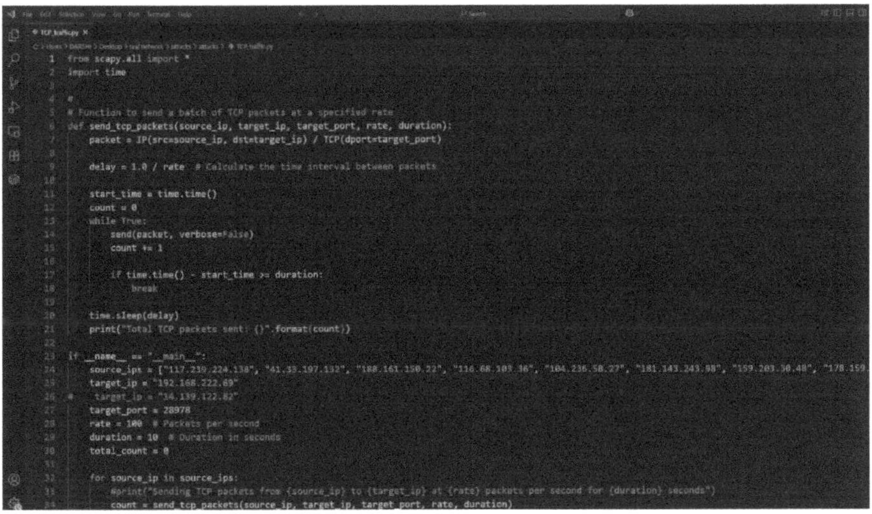

Figure 5.2 TCP flood traffic generation – Scapy Script

5.3. Simulation of Volumetric DDoS attacks on controlled Environment

In this section, we defined implementation of the experiment and execution of the experiment we carried out in controlled environment. In this experiment, volumetric DDoS attack simulation was performed over virtual machines connected to different virtual networks.

5.3.1. Experimental Environment

In the experimental environment, two virtual machines were deployed with isolated network configurations. VM1 was assigned to Virtual Network A, while VM2 was assigned to Virtual Network B, ensuring network-level separation between the instances.

For this experiment implementation, we set up three virtual machines through Virtual Box with a Linux-based operating system (ubuntu) on two machines and a Windows machine. All three virtual machines were deployed with isolated network configurations. Virtual machine 1 (system A) was part of Virtual Network A. Virtual Machine 2 (system B) was part of Virtual Network B. and Virtual Machine C mainly intended for generating attack traffic was assigned to Virtual Machine C. These Virtual machines were configured a separate network segment and restricted level 1 and level 2 connectivity. Each virtual machine had reasonable internet connectivity and necessary network tools named Wireshark and Snort as an IDS/ IPS at the internet gateway, and the default firewall. we carried out this experiment on a PC with Intel (R) Core (TM) i5-5200U CPU @ 2.20GHz 2.20 GHz and 8 GB RAM (Patel, Darshi, 2024). Additionally, the POLY-DDOSCHAIN DApps became interface between Intra-domain mitigation scheme and Collaborative mitigation scheme by providing web-based interface.

5.3.2. Experiment Execution Details

We simulated a volumetric DDoS attack (UDP, TCP and ICMP flood attacks) on system A (victim) for 10 minutes without implementing the proposed solution. And we collected the network logs and measured statistics, results. Afterwards, to measure the effectiveness of the proposed solution, we simulated a volumetric DDoS attack on system A for 10 minutes with the proposed solution. For that, system A was registered in the proposed DApps - POLY-DDOSCHAIN and implemented the proposed solution. The attack was detected at system A's end and get blocked the attack through the proposed solution, and then a snort-generated file of suspicious IP addresses and attack signatures was reported through the addIpfsHashStorage smart contract through the proposed DApps - POLY-DDOSCHAIN. Figure 5.3 shows addIpfsHashStorage Smart contract code written in Remix IDE. We measured the result for System A (victim collaborator or reporter collaborator). Then we simulated the same volume-based flooding DDoS attack on System B (receiver collaborator) for the same time and intensity where System B is already a collaborator of the proposed solution and already performed mitigation action according to the reported file (reported by victim collaborator System A) and measured the network logs and results. We have taken some parts of this text from our previously published research work (Patel, Darshi, 2024).

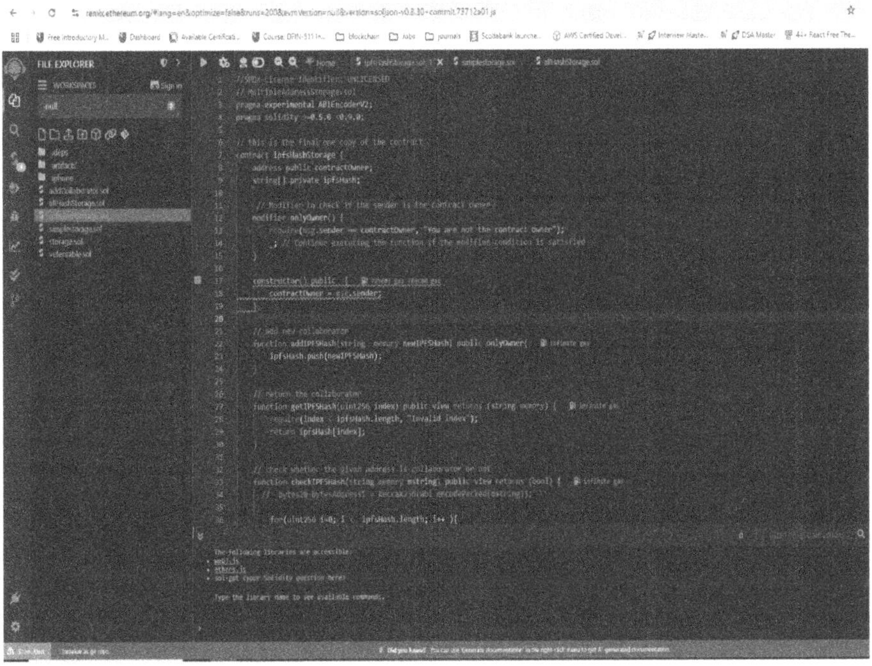

Figure 5.3. addIpfsHashStorage Smart Contract code – Remix IDE

Experimental result, statistics and analysis of this experiment are briefly provided in the Chapter 6.

5.4. Simulation of Volumetric DDoS attacks on Distributed Network

This section described implementation of the experiment and its execution and overview of emulator we used for simulation of this experiment. This experiment aimed to validate the proposed solution in distributed environment, where this solution worked as open, transparent collaborator among distributed networks. In this experiment, volumetric DDoS attack performed over distributed networks which facilitated by Mininet Emulator (*Mininet Walkthrough - Mininet*, n.d.).

5.4.1. Mininet Emulator

Mininet is a lightweight network emulator, mainly used to create a realistic virtual network. Mininet can run real kernel, switch, controller, links and application source code on top of a realistic virtual network through single machine. This single machine can be virtual machine, cloud or native. It mainly utilized lightweight virtualization to emulate the network environment. The main use case of Mininet is development and testing of Software Defined Networking (SDN) related applications and functionalities and SDN. Additionally, Mininet is also used for testing and validation of network protocol without implementing it on physical hardware or network devices. Mininet provides realistic view of network so protocol testing and SDN based deployment become efficient without explicitly relay on physical network infrastructure. Mininet also provides interactive Command line interface (CLI) and Graphical User Interface (GUI) to connect with the emulated network, along with that customization and sharing with other tools and networks makes it a perfect choice for development, educational and research. This emulated deployment tested over Mininet can be easily and efficiently deploy over real network or real hardware infrastructure, differentiates Mininet from other network emulators.

In Mininet, hosts run standard Linux network software, and its switches support OpenFlow for highly flexible custom routing and SDN. It also supports system-level regression tests, development of arbitrary custom topologies and provide extensive support of Python API integration for emulation of networks and experiments. Mininet utilized process-based virtualization instead of process abstraction (mainly run by Operating system) for virtualize hosts and network components run over a single physical Operating system. Mininet is Linux based and written in python other than some C utilities. Mininet contains many best features and functionalities of emulators, simulators such as without full system virtualization provides more bandwidth, fast, largely scaled network devices, quickly reconfigurable network infrastructure without physical devices, and efficient in terms of real network connection, with interactive performance to network devices (*Mininet Walkthrough - Mininet*, n.d.). On Contrary, Mininet cannot support non-Linux compatible OpenFlow switches or applications, is a limitation of Mininet but in real-time it does not hinder its development. By considering all these functionalities, features of Mininet and evaluating other network emulators such as GNS3 and NetEm, we utilized Mininet to test our proposed solution over distributed network.

5.4.2. Experimental Environment

This experiment was carried out to validate the proposed solution over distributed network. So, in this section, Distributed Network design, experiment set up, proposed solution implementation is defined in detail. From the implementation point of view, experiment was carried out on Mininet environment. Mininet was installed and run on Ubuntu based Virtual Machine.

Distributed Network was designed in Mininet environment. For distributed network design, we configured 10 isolated different networks with different subnets. These isolated 10 different networks communicated to each other through routing. Each network is configured using a /24 subnet, so in each network 254 hosts could be added. In each network, an individual host connected to router of that network via switch. Here we configured only one host per network, but up to 254 hosts can be added upon requirement. Number of hosts in individual network could not change the result of the experiment means result of this experiment is not depended on host count in an individual network. Each network configured through different subnet and communicated through routing fulfill the first condition of distributed network. Additionally, logically separation of each network also considers each network as a part of distributed network. Secondly, a network considers as a distributed when all the participating networks are operated autonomously and no central point of control over them. In this experiment, all networks that form a distributed network were autonomous and no central point of control enforced over the participated networks. Figure 5.4. shows Mininet topology of distributed network where 10 different hosts, switches, controller connected to form network topology and testing of their connections through pingall.

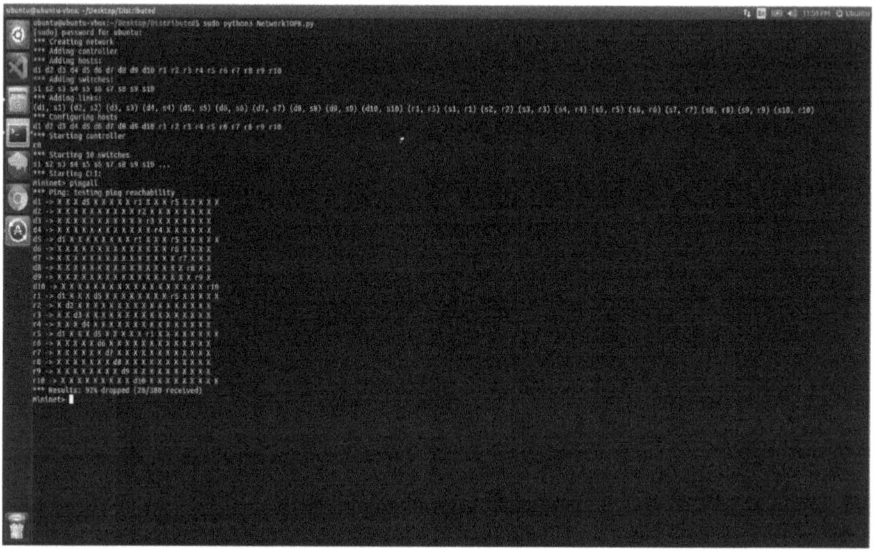

Figure 5.4. Mininet topology defines Distributed Network

In this experiment, each network (node) ran proposed solution for the purpose of volumetric DDoS attacks mitigation. This fulfills shared objective property of distributed network. From implementation perspective, the proposed Intra-network scheme to mitigate volumetric DDoS attack was implemented at network level by running Snort and IP-blocking firewall (Linux) at individual network end (here individual network consider as a collaborator). Additionally, the proposed DApps ran on administrative host level for participation in the proposed collaborative mitigation scheme. Communication between Intra-domain scheme and collaborative scheme was handled through APIs.

Additionally, while creating this Distributed network of 10 different networks, each network was isolated and not connected to each other in any direct or indirect network links or connected not even router to router connectivity. Among these 10 networks, we chose network 1 for attack traffic generation for this experiment. Means collaboration of 9 diverse autonomous networks and 1 attacker network for generating attack towards these networks. This one network utilized various attack traffic generation tools such as hping3 and scapy library to generate attacks traffic from multiple sources towards victim network. This attacker network connected to each network for experimental purpose (to test each network under attack situation and validate proposed solution) for that attacker network and victim network formed connectivity through router, no level 1 or level 2 connectivity exist other than routing.

5.4.3. Experiment Execution Details

This experiment intended to test and validate the proposed solution over distributed network, was carried out in Mininet environment. As mentioned in previous section, all the networks were autonomous and had no connectivity to each other. But for attack traffic generation and testing, we connected Attacker Network (d1) to each remaining networks through routing. We simulated a volumetric DDoS attack (UDP, TCP, ICMP flood attacks) from attacker network (d1) to victim networks d2, d3, d4, and d5 one by one separately for about 10 minutes without implementing proposed solution. And we collected network logs and measured statistics, results.

Then after, to validate the proposed solution in terms of attacks mitigation, we simulated a volumetric DDoS attack (UDP, TCP, ICMP flood) for the time duration of about 10 minutes from attacker network (d1) to victim network d2, d3, d4 and d5 one by one respectively with the proposed solution. For that, all other autonomous networks such as d2, d3, d4, d5, d6, d7, d8, d9, d10 were implemented the proposed solution by registering in the proposed system DApps – POLY-DDOSCHAIN. Figure 5.5 shows the proposed system DApps that hosted on web – a web interface. The attack detected at d2 network's end and mitigated through the proposed solution. Simultaneously, a snort-generated blacklisted IP addresses file was reported by invoking addIpfsHashStorage smart contract from the proposed DApps from d2 collaborator's end. We measured the result for d2 collaborator (Victim network). Then we simulated same kind of volumetric DDoS attack on Victim networks d3, d4, d5 from attacker network (d1) for the same time and intensity where these d3, d4, d5 networks already part of proposed collaboration and already changed their mitigation strategies according to the attack signature file (reported by the reporter d2 network). We measured network logs, traces for each network after implementation of the proposed solution.

Figure 5.5 Proposed System DApps - POLY-DDOSCHAIN – Web Interface

Experimental result, statistics and analysis of this experiment are briefly provided in the Chapter 6.

5.5. Simulation of Volumetric DDoS attacks on real Network

In this section, implementation of the experiment and execution details of the experiment we carried out in Real Environment are described. This experiment aimed to validate proposed solution on real network and provide insights on effectiveness of the proposed solution in real time. In this experiment, volumetric DDoS attack simulation was performed over real environment (in controlled manner).

5.5.1. Experimental Environment

This experiment was carried out to validate the proposed solution over real network. But before providing experiment setup and execution details, several key factors were considered while designing experiment for the real network. Firstly, according to Information Technology Act, 2000, simulating DDoS over real network without proper permission is illegitimate. Additionally, many organizations even don't provide permission to simulate DDoS attacks on their production or public network. Majority of research study related to DDoS attacks related solutions have been tested on simulators or controlled testbed. So, after considering all these factors, we chose to simulate volumetric DDoS attacks over controlled real environment of Gujarat

Vidyapith Network, where we could simulate controlled volumetric DDoS attacks and validate our proposed solution.

This experiment was carried out in a LAN of Gujarat Vidyapith Network, where we utilized total three hosts of LAN to execute this experiment. Thie experiment was carried out with considering all the security and operational factors of the network. This experiment was conducted without disrupting legitimate operation of other LAN users and without causing unintended damage to network and resources. For that, we simulated low rate (low intensity) of volumetric DDoS attacks over real LAN, just enough to trigger detection, mitigation and fulfill proposed system validation/testing goal.

In this experiment, One LAN host was dedicated for generating attacks traffic called attacker host (system 3) towards two other hosts. This system 3 utilized various attack traffic generation tools such as hping3 and scapy library to generate attacks traffic from multiple sources towards other systems. As we conducted this experiment over LAN, we pressured that host 1 (system 1) and host 2 (system 2) were not communicated directly through routing or level 1 or level 2 connection. Each system participated in this experiment had reasonable internet connectivity and necessary network tools named Wireshark, Snort as an IDS/IPS and the default firewall (windows). This system 1 and system 2 acted as a collaborator in this experiment after registration in the proposed system DApps. And the POLY-DDOSCHAIN DApps interfaced between Intra-domain scheme and Collaborative mitigation scheme by proving web-based interface.

5.5.2. Experiment Execution Details

The main objective of this experiment was to test and validate the proposed solution over real network, as we discussed earlier, we chose to execute this experiment over controlled real environment of Gujarat Vidyapith Network. This experiment was carried out in LAN of Gujarat Vidyapith Network because of legal and administrative concerns.

We choose three distinct systems of a LAN utilized for execution of this experiment. First, we simulated a volumetric DDoS attack (UDP, TCP and ICMP flood attacks) on system 1 for about 10 minutes without implementing the proposed solution. Attack traffic generation task was performed by the system 3 (attacker), where different traffic generation software and scripts generated diverse network traffic. Various network logs and statistics were collected and measured for this. Afterwards, by enabling the proposed solution on system 1, we again simulated a volumetric DDoS attack on system 1 for about 10 minutes and measured system logs and statistics. For enabling the proposed solution at system 1's end, the system 1 first registered in the proposed DApps – POLY-DDOSCHAIN and implemented the proposed solution. After enabling the proposed solution, a volumetric DDoS attacks detected and mitigated at system 1's end through Intra-domain mitigation scheme. Simultaneously, as part of collaborative mitigation scheme, a Snort-generated file which contained blacklisted IP addresses generated at system 1's end and reposted to other collaborators through the proposed DApps by invoking the addIpfsHashStorage smart contract. All network logs and statistics were measured from system 1 for this instance. Figure 5.6 shows Network Logs and Packet Analysis Interface of Wireshark.

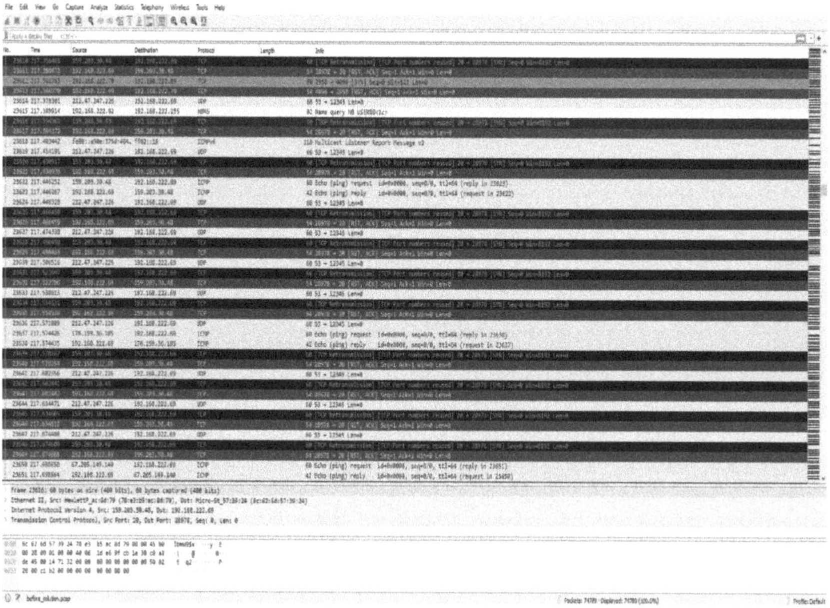

Figure 5.6. Wireshark – Network Logs and Packet Analysis Interface

Then we simulated the similar volume-based flooding DDoS attack on system 2 (receiver collaborator) for the same time and intensity where System 2 was already a collaborator of the proposed solution and implemented attack mitigation actions according to the attack signature file (reported by victim collaborator system 1). We also measured the network logs and results for this instance from system 2. Snort generated Blacklisted IP address File which contains malicious IP addresses detected during volumetric attack detection by Snort is shown in Figure 5.7.

78.96.190.54
91.109.190.5
91.109.186.7
46.30.45.154
162.220.166.114
91.109.184.3
116.202.101.219
1.47.234.183
91.109.182.3
91.109.182.8
188.168.107.194
217.165.164.110
91.109.188.4
113.140.6.198
115.76.136.72
117.199.12.148
78.97.110.47
86.98.145.152
79.139.144.107
186.49.246.187
91.109.186.3
89.137.162.193
46.153.99.185
186.49.247.123
151.80.9.113
116.203.151.240
111.88.27.40
36.4.183.52
182.187.71.101
60.169.115.194
95.71.249.141

Figure 5.7 Snort generated Blacklisted IP address File

In this chapter, we briefly discussed implementation of the proposed solution. For validation and testing of the proposed solution, various experiments were carried out in different network environments. This proposed solution was tested, validated over Controlled environment, distributed network and real network. These experimentation details provide brief idea about proposed solution's applicability and integration of proposed solution to various networks without significant modification of proposed solution. This defines implementation flexibility and simplicity of proposed solution compared to other collaborative solutions.

CHAPTER 6: RESULTS AND DISCUSSIONS

After completing implementation and validation part of the proposed system in previous chapter, this chapter elaborates result and evaluation of the proposed solution. Firstly, Experimental results of the experiments carried out on different environments such as controlled environment, Distributed Network and Real Network are presented and discussed in detail. After that, the next section shows performance Evaluation of the proposed solution. Finally, this chapter comes to an end of the discussion by presenting conclusion and future direction of the proposed solution.

6.1. Experimental Results

This section is dedicated to representing experimental results of the proposed system. The results of experiments which carried out for the purpose of validation and testing of the proposed solution in various environments are briefly discussed by presenting various network graphs and statistics.

6.1.1. Simulation of Volumetric DDoS attacks on controlled Environment – Experiment Results

Experimental results of the experiment where we simulated volumetric DDoS attacks on controlled environment are defined and discussed in this section. This experiment was carried out on the controlled environment of various virtual networks set up over virtual machines. This experiment aimed to validate and test the proposed solution deployed over controlled environment to mitigate volumetric DDoS attacks. The following part of this section is taken from our previous publication (Patel, Darshi, 2024).

Firstly, without enabling the proposed solution on System A, Volumetric DDoS attacks (TCP, UDP, ICMP flood) targeted over System A for about 10 minutes with around 5040 packets per minutes intensity. As effect of this attack on System, an average 90 to 95 packets per second (pps) rate is observed with a TCP error rate between 20 to 30 pps, shown in Figure. 6.1, which clearly indicates that system A had become the victim of a volumetric DDoS attack and system performance is also downgraded. Then to validate the proposed solution, we simulated the same kind of volumetric attacks on System A after enabling the proposed solution. As result, the volumetric DDoS attack detected and mitigated through the proposed solution (Intra-network mitigation scheme), then after System A reported the attacks to other collaborators (as part of collaborative mitigation scheme) by sharing blacklisted IP addresses and attack signatures file through the proposed DApps - POLY-DDOSCHAIN.

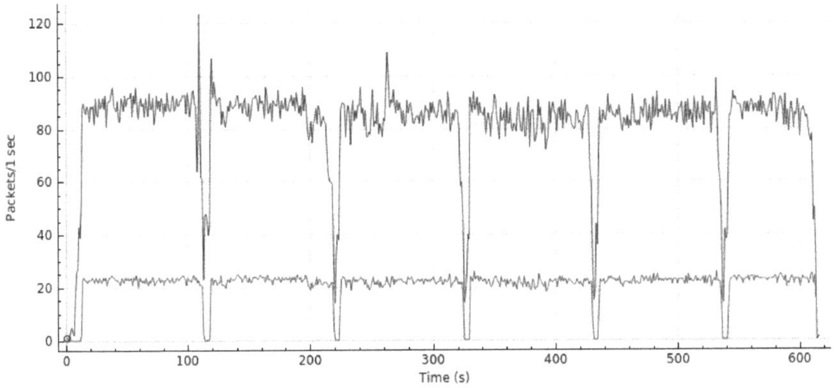

Figure: 6.1. I/O Graph of Volumetric DDoS attacks on System A when the proposed solution is disabled.

Note: - Here Black line indicates overall traffic and blue line indicates TCP errors.

For the purpose of testing the proposed solution from collaborative perspective (means other collaborators in the proposed system able to mitigate the attacks which detected by System A), we simulated the same kind of volumetric DDoS attacks with same attack intensity for about 10 minutes on another system in collaboration named System B after enabling the proposed solution. Recorded results of this experiment shows that average 8 to 12 pps is detected after enabling the proposed solution, with negligible TCP error rates around 1 to 2 pps, which is significantly less compared to System A. These packets per second rates (pps) and TCP error rates of the System B after enabling the proposed system is defined in Figure 6.2. This result indicates that volumetric DDoS attacks that targeted System B (receiver node) have no impact on System B after enabling the proposed solution. Attack traffic was blocked in advance before the attack was performed on System B, and prevention measures were helpful to sustain system performance in under-attack situations due to the proposed solution.

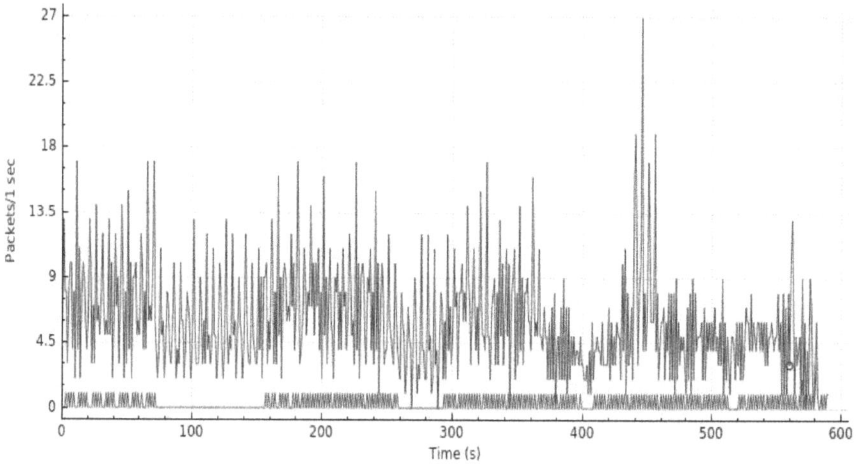

Figure: 6.2. I/O Graph of Volumetric DDoS attacks on System B when the proposed Solution is enabled.

Note: - Here Black line indicates overall traffic and blue line indicates TCP errors.

While comparing packets per second rate, System A's pps rate is about nine times higher than System B's pps rate. System A's pps rate is significantly high due to attack traffic, whereas System B's packets per second rate is normal. Only legitimate traffic was traversed to the network after blocking illegitimate IP addresses reported through the proposed solution, as depicted in Figures 6.1 and 6.2. The TCP error rate indicates the performance of the system, so at the time of the attack, the TCP error rate is around 22 pps and two pps for System A and System B, respectively, which means System B can be able to serve more numbers of legitimate requests under attack conditions.

System statistics for both systems are given in Table 6.1. revealing that attack traffic is completely blocked at System B after implementing the proposed solution. It is observed by the total number of packets captured and blacklisted and dropped packets. The packets-per-minute rate of both systems indicates that volumetric DDoS attacks were mitigated on System B after enabling the proposed solution in advance.

	Total Number of Packets captured	Total Number of Blacklisted IPs Blocked	Total Number of Packets Blacklisted by Snort & dropped by firewall	Packets per Minute Rate
System A without the proposed solution	50337	0	0	5032
System B with the proposed solution	50534	6568	46642	389

[Table 6.1: System Statistics – Experiment performed over Controlled Environment]

6.1.2. Simulation of Volumetric DDoS attacks on Distributed Network – Experiment Results

In this section, Experimental results of the experiment where we simulated volumetric DDoS attacks on Distributed network environment are defined and discussed in detail. This experiment was carried out on the distributed network which was emulated by utilizing Mininet Emulator. This experiment aimed to validate and test the proposed solution deployed over distributed network environment to mitigate volumetric DDoS attacks.

The experiment implementation details for this simulation of volumetric DDoS attack over Distributed Network to validate the proposed solution are given in previous chapter. Volumetric DDoS attacks (TCP, UDP, ICMP flood) attack simulated over different isolated networks that formed a distributed environment to validate and test the proposed solution over distributed environment through Mininet simulator. First, Volumetric DDoS attacks simulated on isolated network d2 (Reporter network / system) without enabling the proposed solution for about 10 minutes and measured the results. The d2 network / system became victim of the volumetric DDoS attack depicted from the system statistics and network logs as shown in table 6.2 and Figure 6.3. Then after, enabling the proposed solution, we again simulated the same kind of attack on d2 network for about 10 minutes and recorded the results. The proposed solution blocked and mitigated the attack by utilizing Intra-network attack mitigation scheme shown in

Figure 6.4. As d2 was a Reporter system, D2 reported the blacklisted IP address file which generated as a product of attack mitigation to other collaborators (d3, d4, d5, d6, d7, d8, d9, d10) in the distributed network, this sharing of attack signature file considered as a part of collaborative mitigation scheme. Among these 10 isolated networks, experiment was carried out over some selected systems (d3, d4, d5) which acts as a collaborator system other than d2 (the reporter system).

	Total Number of Packets captured	Inbound	Outbound	Normal traffic	Total Number of Blacklisted IPs Blocked
System d2 without Proposed solution	45736	28924	16737	75	0
System d2 with Proposed solution	26663	26572	51	40	60

[Table 6.2: System Statistics – Experiment performed over Distributed Network – System d2 (Reporter System)]

Results and statistics of simulation of volumetric DDoS attack performed over Reporter system d2 without enabling the proposed solution and after enabling the proposed solution. The Table 6.2 shows the some of the statistics which captured during the experiment on Reporter System d2. Total captured packets, inbound and outbound traffic indicates that attack traffic completely blocked by the proposed solution, which originated from the 60 attackers' IP addresses.

Attack duration – about 10 minutes

Attack Type – TCP, UDP, and ICMP Flood

Distributed Network (System) – d2 (Reporter system)

Note: - Here Red line indicates Inbound traffic and black line indicates Outbound traffic.

- **Inbound and Outbound Packets per Second Rate**

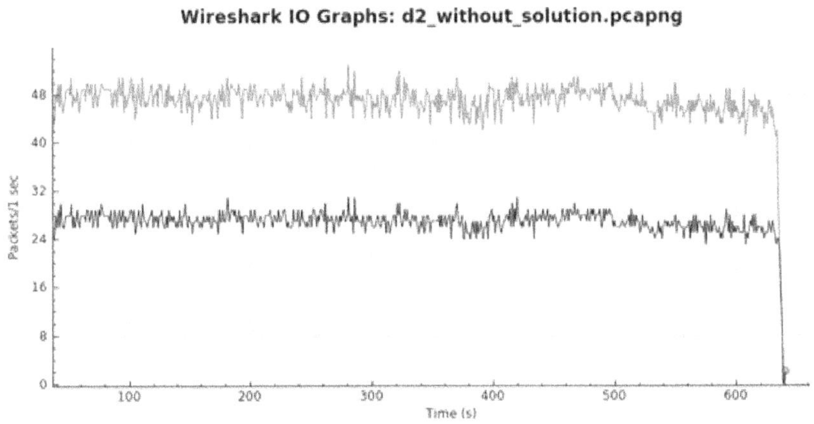

Figure: 6.3. I/O Graph of Volumetric DDoS attacks on System d2 when the proposed Solution is disabled.

- **Inbound and Outbound Packets per Second Rate**

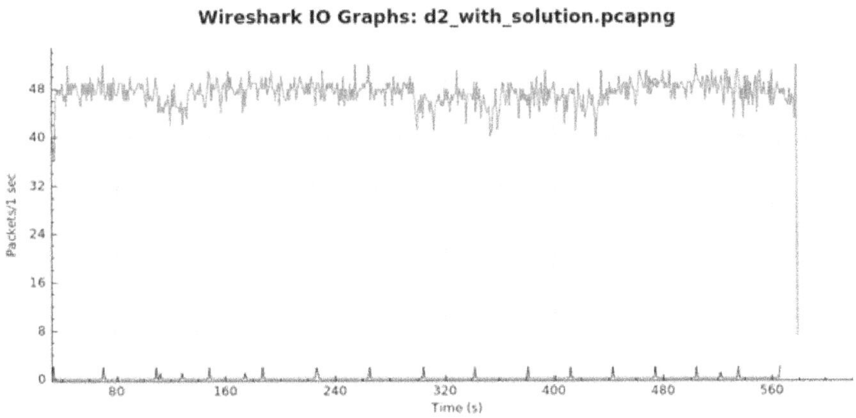

Figure: 6.4. I/O Graph of Volumetric DDoS attacks on System d2 when the proposed Solution is enabled.

Analysis: -

1. Inbound traffic of System d2 fluctuates in range of 36 pps to 52 pps and outbound traffic of System d2 was in range of 22 pps to 30 when proposed solution is disabled.

Whereas Inbound traffic was reported in range of 36 pps to 52 pps and outbound traffic was in range of 0 to 4 on System d2 after enabling the proposed solution.

2. After enabling the proposed solution, when attack traffic detected (means inbound traffic shown in figure 6.3), Reporter system d2 already blocked the origin of the volumetric attack, so Reporter system d2, was not responding to the attack traffic which is observed from the outbound traffic of I/O graph shown in figure 6.4 (only serving normal traffic).
3. After carefully evaluation of the I/O graphs of Reporter system d2, it is stated that the volumetric DDoS attacks completely blocked and mitigated at Reporter system's end after enabling the proposed collaborative solution.

This experiment carried out over different systems of distributed network for the intention of testing the proposed solution in distributed environment and to measure effectiveness of proposed solution to collaboratively mitigate volumetric DDoS attacks. Volumetric DDoS attack simulated over other isolated networks other than Reporter System of distributed system such as d3, d4, d5 without proposed solution and with proposed solution are defined in below. Additionally, system statistics, result and analysis of each simulation are also discussed in detail.

System statistics and I/O graphs of Collaborator system d5 after Reporter System d2 reported the volumetric DDoS attacks

Attack duration – about 10 minutes

Attack Type – TCP, UDP, and ICMP Flood

Distributed Network (System) – d5 (Collaborator system)

	Total Number of Packets captured	Inbound	Outbound	Normal traffic	Total Number o Blackliste IPs Blocke
System d5 without Proposed solution	43132	27421	15634	77	0
System d5 with Proposed solution	29071	28959	57	55	60

[Table 6.3: System Statistics – Experiment performed over Distributed Network – System d5 (Collaborator System)]

Some system statistics of the Collaborator system d5 was captured in two different scenarios such as without enabling the proposed solution and after enabling the proposed solution shown in Table 6.3. At System d5, before enabling the proposed solution, about 15634 outbound packets were captured. And only 57 outbound packets were observed after enabling the proposed solution. It clearly indicates that total number of attacks originated IP addresses are blocked to mitigate volumetric DDoS attacks, these IP addresses reported by the Reporter system d2 as part of proposed collaborative mitigation scheme. Additionally, System d5 became unresponsive to volumetric attack after enabling the proposed solution and served the normal traffic as usual.

- **Inbound and Outbound Packets per Second Rate**

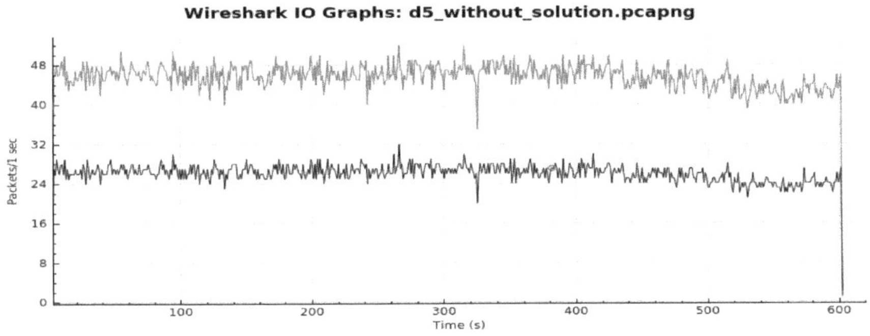

Figure: 6.5. I/O Graph of Volumetric DDoS attacks on System d5 when the proposed Solution is disabled.

- **Inbound and Outbound Packets per Second Rate**

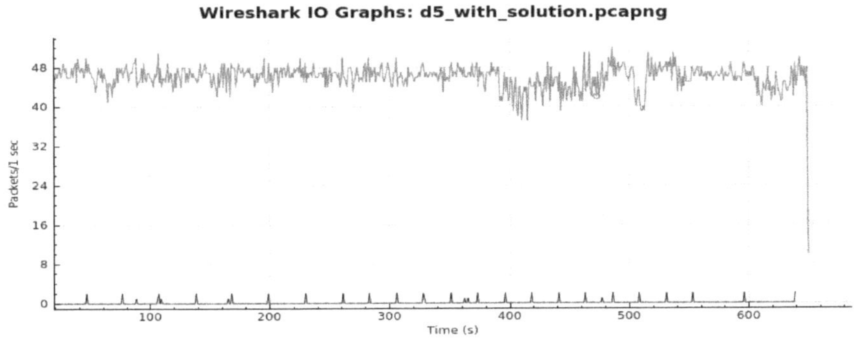

Figure: 6.6. I/O Graph of Volumetric DDoS attacks on System d5 when the proposed Solution is enabled.

Analysis:-

1. Inbound traffic of System d5 fluctuates in range of 34 pps to 52 pps and outbound traffic of System d5 is in range of 20 pps to 32 when proposed solution is disabled. Whereas Inbound traffic is reported in range of 36 pps to 54 pps and outbound traffic is in range of 0 to 4 on System D5 after enabling the proposed solution.
2. From these two I/O graphs Figure 6.5 and Figure 6.6, it is observed that Outbound traffic after enabling the proposed solution significantly reduced in System d5 compared to before enabling the proposed solution. This shows that System already blocked the illegitimates IP addresses caused for the volumetric attack before the attacks. (attack detected and reported by Reported system d2). And system become unresponsive to volumetric attack.
3. After carefully evaluation of the I/O graphs of Collaborator system d5, it is stated that the volumetric DDoS attacks completely blocked and mitigated at Collaborator system's end after enabling the proposed collaborative solution.

System statistics and I/O graphs of Collaborator system d4 after Reporter System d2 reported the volumetric DDoS attacks

Attack duration – about 10 minutes

Attack Type – TCP, UDP, and ICMP Flood

Distributed Network (System) – d4 (Collaborator system)

	Total Number of Packets captured	**Inbound**	**Outbound**	**Normal traffic**	**Total Number of Blacklisted IPs Blocked**
System d4 without Proposed solution	40420	25679	14662	79	0
System d4 with Proposed solution	26010	25940	36	34	60

[Table 6.4: System Statistics – Experiment performed over Distributed Network – System d4 (Collaborator System)]

Table 6.4 shows some System Statistics collected during the experiment on System d4. Various statistics such as total number of packets, Inbound packets, outbound packets and normal traffic packets details are extracted from the network traces for observation and evaluation. It is observed that total number of packets and outbound packets in d4 with proposed solution are significantly less compared to total number of packets and outbound packets observed in System d4 without proposed solution. Additionally, System d4 blocked Illegitimate 60 IP addresses as source of the attacks as part of attack mitigation (detected and reported by Reporter system d2) after enabling the proposed solution. The system statistics of System d4 defines that proposed solution blocked the attack effectively and in advance in collaborative System d4's end.

- **Inbound and Outbound Packets per Second Rate**

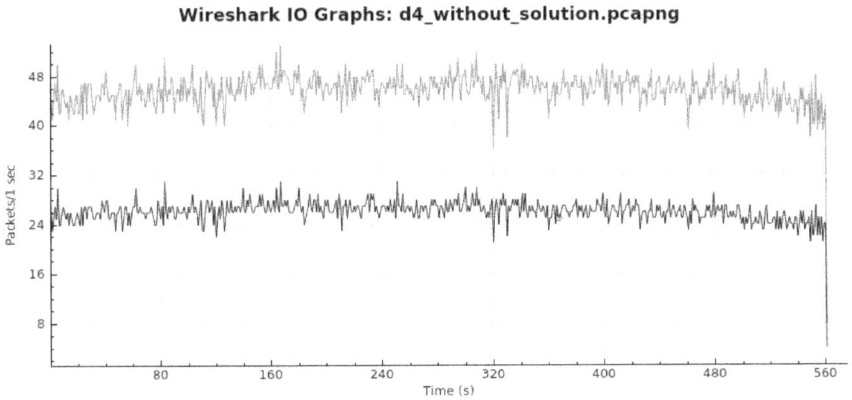

Figure: 6.7. I/O Graph of Volumetric DDoS attacks on System d4 when the proposed Solution is disabled.

- **Inbound and Outbound Packets per Second Rate**

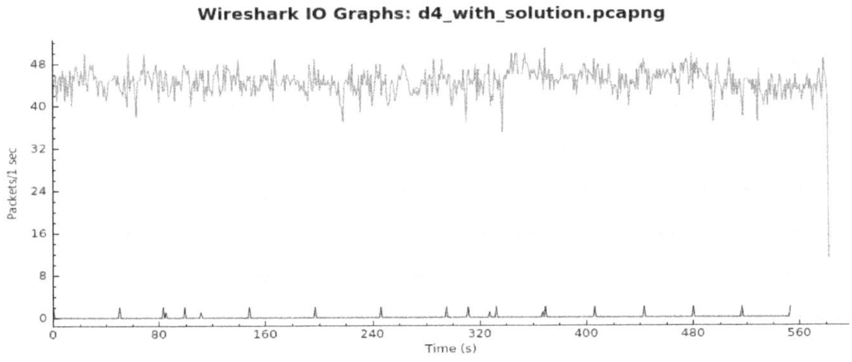

Figure: 6.8. I/O Graph of Volumetric DDoS attacks on System d4 when the proposed Solution is enabled.

Analysis:-

1. Inbound traffic of System d4 fluctuates in range of 34 pps to 52 pps and outbound traffic of System d4 is in range of 20 pps to 30 when proposed solution is disabled, as shown in Figure 6.7. Whereas as per Figure 6.8, Inbound traffic is reported in range of 34 pps to 50 pps and outbound traffic is in range of 0 to 4 on System d4 after enabling the proposed solution.
2. The inbound traffic at System d4 indicates that volumetric DDoS traffic observed at d4 but after enabling the proposed solution, System d4 hasn't responded to this inbound traffic requests, which is clearly observed from the difference in Outbound traffic of the I/O graphs.
3. After evaluating both I/O graphs, it is stated that Volumetric DDoS attack traffic efficiently blocked and mitigated at Collaborator System d4, without taking any additional overhead of attack detection as already detected attack information shared by the Reporter system d4.

System statistics and I/O graphs of Collaborator system d3 after Reporter System d2 reported the volumetric DDoS attacks

Attack duration – about 10 minutes

Attack Type – TCP, UDP, and ICMP Flood

Distributed Network (System) – d3 (Collaborator system)

	Total Number of Packets captured	Inbound	Outbound	Normal traffic	Total Number of Blacklisted IPs Blocked
System d3 without Proposed solution	44691	28319	16228	72	0
System d3 with Proposed solution	27258	27152	54	52	60

[Table 6.5: System Statistics – Experiment performed over Distributed Network – System d3 (Collaborator System)]

Some system statistics of the Collaborator system d3 was captured in two different scenarios such as without enabling the proposed solution and after enabling the proposed solution shown in Table 6.5. At System d3, before enabling the proposed solution, about 16228 outbound packets were captured. And only 54 outbound packets were observed after enabling the proposed solution. It clearly indicates that total number of attacks originated IP addresses are blocked to mitigate volumetric DDoS attacks, these IP addresses reported by the Reporter system d2 as part of proposed collaborative mitigation scheme. Moreover, System d3 became unresponsive to volumetric attack after enabling the proposed solution and served the normal traffic as usual.

- **Inbound and Outbound Packets per Second Rate**

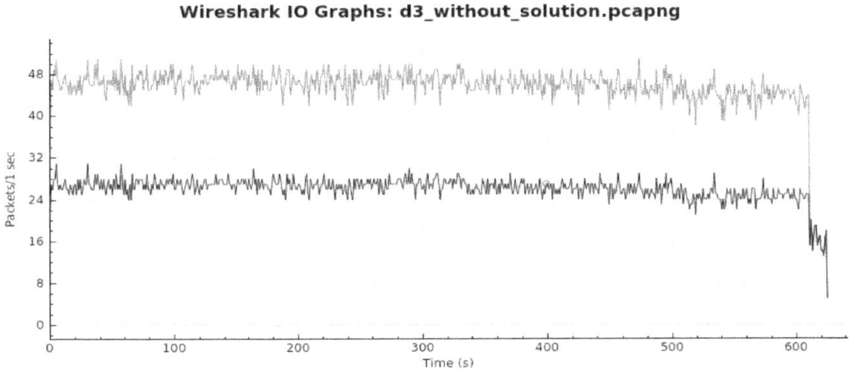

Figure: 6.9. I/O Graph of Volumetric DDoS attacks on System d3 when the proposed Solution is disabled.

- **Inbound and Outbound Packets per Second Rate**

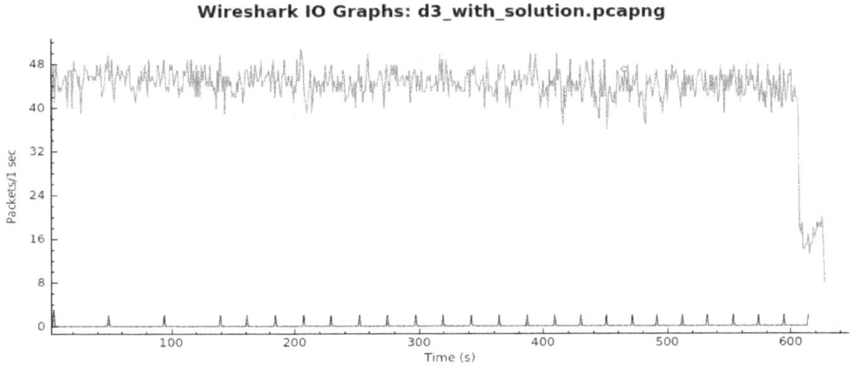

Figure: 6.10. I/O Graph of Volumetric DDoS attacks on System d3 when the proposed Solution is enabled.

Analysis: -

1. According to I/O graph shown in Figure 6.9, Inbound traffic of System D3 fluctuates in range of 38 pps to 52 pps and outbound traffic of System d3 is in range of 22 pps to 32 when proposed solution is disabled. Whereas Inbound traffic is reported in range of 36 pps to 50 pps and outbound traffic is in range of 0 to 4 on System D3 after enabling the proposed solution as defined in Figure 6.10.
2. After enabling the proposed solution, when attack traffic detected (means inbound traffic shown in figure 6.9), Collaborator system d3 already blocked the origin of the volumetric attack as reported by Reporter system d2, so collaborator system d3, was not responding to the attack traffic which is observed from the outbound traffic of I/O graph shown in figure 6.10 (only serving normal traffic). This indicates that attacks prevention and mitigation at Collaborative system d3's end, as attack detection and signaled by Reporter system d2 through the proposed solution collaboratively.
3. After carefully evaluation of the I/O graphs of Collaborator system d3, it is stated that the volumetric DDoS attacks completely blocked and mitigated at Reporter system's end after enabling the proposed collaborative solution.

6.1.3. Simulation of Volumetric DDoS attacks on Real Network – Experiment Results

This section discusses experimental results of the Simulation of volumetric DDoS attacks on Real network. The experiment implementation details provided in the previous chapter, where experiment was carried out controlled real environment of Gujarat Vidyapith Network. The main objective of this experiment is to validate and test the proposed collaborative solution over real network and provides complete details of the proposed solution from implementation perspective.

This experiment was carried out over a LAN of Gujarat Vidyapith Network without disrupting the legitimate traffic flow of the network. Three different hosts of the LAN were utilized to perform this experiment. Volumetric DDoS attacks (UDP, TCP and ICMP flood) traffic generated for about 10 minutes from one of the hosts named System 3 towards Victim host – System 1 without implementing the proposed solution. As result of the attack, Total 73099 packets were recorded, with Inbound and Outbound traffic of about 40984 and 24231 packets respectively. The results and system statistics extracted from the network logs and traces are given in Table 6.6, Figure 6.11, and Figure 6.12. Then after, to validate and test the proposed solution, we implemented the proposed solution over System 1 and again simulated the Volumetric DDoS attack for 10 minutes on System 1 and measured the result. As the proposed solution enabled on System 1, the Volumetric DDoS attacks detected and System 1 shared blacklisted IP address file (which contains attacker's IP addresses, detected by the proposed solution) through the proposed DApps to other collaborators in the proposed solution. System 1 reported 62 attacker's IP addresses as detected during attack by Intra-domain mitigation scheme of the proposed solution.

Afterwards, the Volumetric DDoS attack (TCP, UDP and ICMP flood) was simulated over System 2 after enabling the proposed solution. Network traces and logs were captured during the attack on System 2. As Attack details and IP addresses already reported by System 1 in the proposed solution, System 2, already blocked these blacklisted IP addresses, which is defined in Table 6.6. Additionally, Total number of packets captured during the attack on System 2 was 49236 packets after enabling the proposed solution along with 40220 inbound packets and 107 outbound packets as shown in Table 6.6. The difference in Total number packets and outbound packets between both the System indicates that System 2 completely blocked the Volumetric DDoS attack after enabling the proposed solution, as attack detected and reported by System 1 beforehand. Figure 6.13 and Figure 6.14 also shown that attack traffic was completely blocked and mitigated at System 2's end after enabling the proposed solution, overall packets rate and Outbound traffic of System 2 implicitly defines this. Repeatedly attack detection overhead at Collaborator System 2 level was avoided and System 2 was serving the normal traffic during the under-attack scenario without performance degradation.

Attack duration – 10 minutes

Attack Type – TCP, UDP, and ICMP Flood

Real Network (System) – LAN (System 1)

	Total Number of Packets Captured	Inbound	Outbound	Normal traffic and other traffic	Total Number Blacklis IPs Bloc
System 1 without Praposed solution	73099	40984	24231	7884	0
System 2 with Praposed Solution	49236	40220	107	8909	62

[Table 6.6: System Statistics – Experiment performed over Gujarat Vidyapith Network (LAN) – Real Environment]

- **Overall Packets per Second Rate**

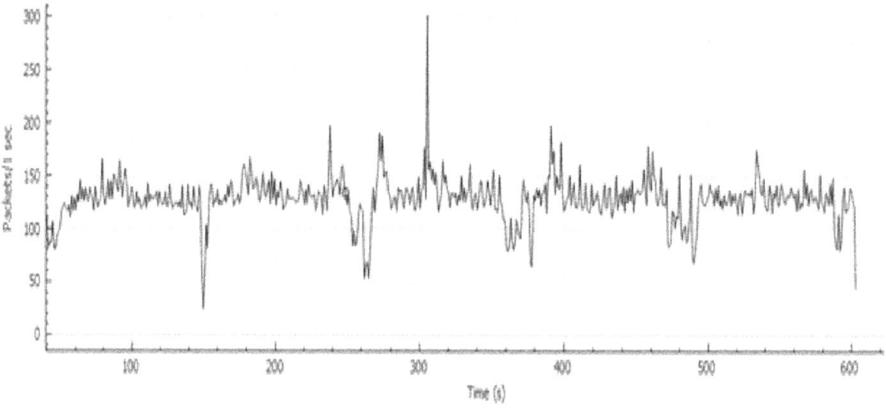

Figure: 6.11. I/O Graph of Volumetric DDoS attacks on System 1 when the proposed Solution is disabled – Overall Packets per second rate.

Note: - Here Black line indicates overall traffic defined in packets per seconds.

- **Inbound and Outbound Packets per Second Rate**

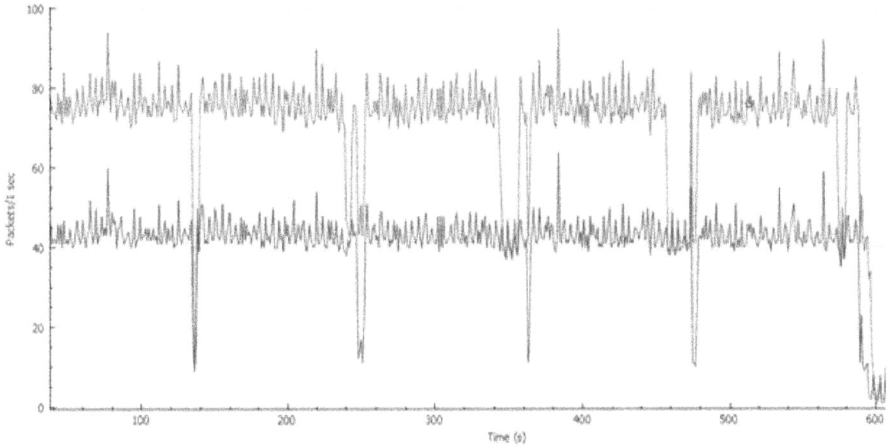

Figure: 6.12. I/O Graph of Volumetric DDoS attacks on System 1 when the proposed Solution is disabled.

Note: - Here Red line indicates Inbound traffic and blue line indicates Outbound traffic.

- **Overall Packets per Second Rate**

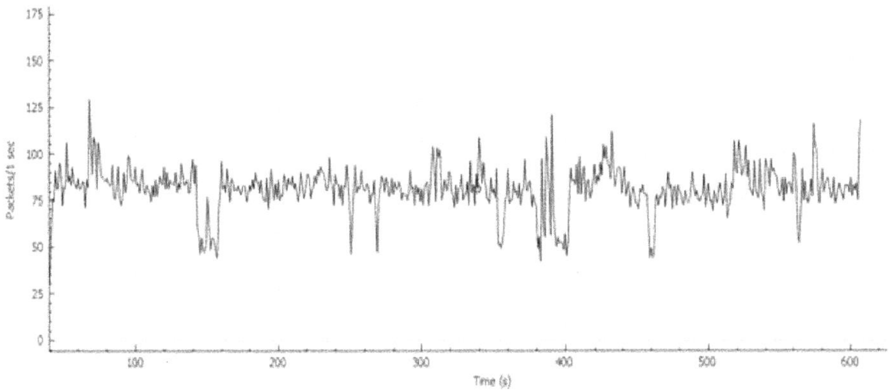

Figure: 6.13. I/O Graph of Volumetric DDoS attacks on System 2 when the proposed Solution is disabled – Overall Packets per second rate.

Note: - Here Black line indicates overall traffic defined in packets per seconds.

- **Inbound and Outbound Packets per Second Rate**

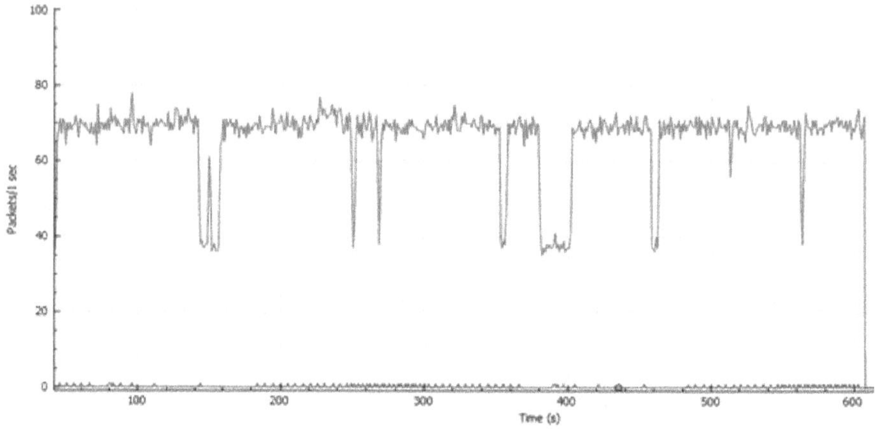

Figure: 6.14. I/O Graph of Volumetric DDoS attacks on System 2 when the proposed Solution is disabled.

Note: - Here Red line indicates Inbound traffic and blue line indicates Outbound traffic.

Analysis:-

1. It is observed that, overall packets rate in System 1 without the proposed solution is observed in range of 25 pps to 300 pps, whereas, after enabling the proposed solution on System 2, overall packets rate is noticed in range of 25 pps to 130 pps. So, it clearly indicates that attack traffic is observed at System 2's end, but as System 2 already blocked the attack sources, System 2 become unresponsive to the attack, which is noticed by half of less of pps rate of System 2 compared to pps rate of System 1 without implementing the proposed solution (Figure 6.11 and Figure 6.13).
2. After carefully observing the Figure 6.12 and Figure 6.14, it is stated that Outbound traffic of the system 1 which describes the response to the attack traffic, is observed in range of 15 pps to 65 pps, while proposed solution is disabled. Whereas after enabling the proposed solution on System 2, outbound traffic is observed in range of 0 to 3. Which means attack traffic is blocked after enabling the blockchain based proposed solution.
3. System 2 was not responding towards the volumetric DDoS attacks during the ongoing attack, after enabling the proposed solution.

6.2. Performance Evaluation

The proposed solution provides Volumetric DDoS attack mitigation collaboratively by utilizing blockchain based architecture. In above section, the experiment results of the three different experiments conducted over different network environment were presented. According to this experiment results, it is clearly observed that the proposed collaborate solution completely blocked the volumetric DDoS attack on collaborative domains after reported attack signature by reporter domain. This experiments results indicates effectiveness and attacks mitigation capability of the proposed solution in collaborative ecosystem.

However, performance measurement and evaluation of proposed solution is crucial because it evaluates the proposed solution over various research objectives and validates it with various parameters. Various performance measurement parameters taken into consideration while evaluating performance of the proposed collaborative solution.

6.2.1. Mitigation Effectiveness

To measure the attack mitigation effectiveness, we took Packets-per-Second (pps) rate and detection overhead of collaborative system. Packets-per-Second (pps) rate is lightweight, real-time observable metric mainly utilized in DDoS attacks and cyber-attacks related research for measuring attack detection and mitigation effectiveness. We utilized pps rate to measure the attack mitigation effectiveness of proposed solution by comparing Outbound pps rate before implementing the proposed solution and after enabling the proposed solution. It is observed that the outbound pps rate of System 2 after implementing the proposed solution is about 27 times lower than System 1's pps rate without enabling the proposed solution (Experiment – Real environment). The same kind of differences in pps rate is observed in other experiments conducted over controlled environment and distributed network. In general, Outbound pps rate is always higher than normal outbound pps rate in under Volumetric DDoS attacks scenario, which observed in many research studies. However, in this research experiments, after implementing the proposed solution, it is observed from all three experiments that outbound pps rate always remain in rage of normal outbound pps rate in under volumetric DDoS attack, that clearly indicates that volumetric DDoS attacks traffic blocked by the proposed solution.

Additionally, attack detection and mitigation overhead of collaborators systems get significantly reduced as attack already reported by the reporter collaborator's system through the proposed collaborative solution. There were no additional attack detection and mitigation measured were taken by the collaborators systems except reported attack information (reported by reporter collaborator system). This clearly indicates that repeated attack detection and mitigation task at other collaborators' end is greatly reduced after implementing the proposed solution, because of collaborative nature of the proposed solution. Moreover, attack detection at single collaborator's end could be beneficial to whole collaboration.

6.2.2. Security

The proposed solution is also evaluated in terms of security. In the proposed solution, attacks signature and information share among other collaborators by utilizing blockchain based architecture. So, the attack information gets secured by default as it inherits the characteristics of blockchain technology. The proposed solution is deployed over Polygon blockchain, and encrypted attack signature files are stored over IPFS, so data integrity and security maintained by default.

Apart from the data security, Blockchain based infrastructure is also secured. As Polygon blockchain utilized Proof-of-Stack (PoS) consensus mechanism and EVM-compatibility provides high security to the Polygon blockchain network and protects the network from the adverse blockchain specific attacks such as "51% attacks" and double-spending attacks. Additionally, Smart Contracts security is taken into the consideration while designing smart contracts of the proposed solution. Smart contracts auditing and security testing tools such as MythX and Remix IDE plugin (security analyzer) were used for vulnerability and security testing of Smart contracts of the proposed System.

6.2.3. Execution Time (Transaction Processing Time)

Execution time or transaction processing time is one of the crucial performance matrices in blockchain related research. In general, (in blockchain ecosystem), Transaction processing time refers to the total amount of time a blockchain takes from transaction submission to confirmed transaction inclusion in the blockchain ledger. In this research, we consider total time the Polygon TestNet – Mumbai TestNet takes to process, confirm and inclusion in Polygon's Mumbai TestNet. Transaction processing Time calculated by combining four different times such as transaction propagation time, Mempool waiting time, Block inclusion time and Finality time, defined in Table 6.7.

- Transaction Propagation time – Time a transaction takes to reach most of the network. In short, time a transaction takes to broadcast to other peer nodes in the distributed network.
- Mempool waiting time – Total time a transaction queued in mempool before inclusion into a block (a miner or validator generally pick a transaction from Mempool).
- Block inclusion time – a total time taken for transaction to be included in a block. (mainly depends on various factors such as block size, Gas fees, network congestion etc).
- Finality time – a time after which a transaction marked as a confirmed. After this time transaction become irreversible and final.

Phase	**Mumbai TestNet**
Transaction Propagation time	~ 1 - 2 s
Mempool waiting time	< ~1 - 5 s
Block inclusion time	~2 s
Finality time	~ 3 - 7 s
Transaction Processing Time (Execution time)	7 s - 16 s

Table 6.7. Transaction processing Time calculation

Note - This Transaction Processing Timings varies based on the time of day, network conditions, and gas fees (these timings were noted on Aug-25-2023 01:05:37 PM +UTC)

In this research, we consider the total time the proposed solution takes after uploading the attack signature file to proposed DApps to the time all the collaborators get this attack signature file. We calculated the Transaction Processing Time by Transaction confirmed time – Transaction submitted time. The execution time of the proposed solution is around less than 14.94 seconds because even the transaction is not confirmed, but still the transaction becomes accessible to over the blockchain. The transaction processing time in TestNet usually higher compared to Mainnet.

Additionally, block size, Gas fees, network congestion are also the significant factors that affects the Transaction Processing Time.

Moreover, we also validated our proposed solution by comparing with the existing solution named BLOSS that utilized blockchain for attack mitigation purpose. BLOSS utilized Ethereum blockchain to signalize the attack and deployed its blockchain based solution on Rinkeby TestNet (*Latest Blocks - ETHEREUM - Rinkeby | BlockExplorer*, n.d.), an Ethereum's official TestNet. The Transaction Processing Time comparison are shown in Figure 6.15. It clearly indicates that the proposed system takes less time transaction processing time compared to BLOSS, because the proposed solution designed using Polygon blockchain. And Polygon, a layer-2 solution has achieved high transaction processing time than Ethereum.

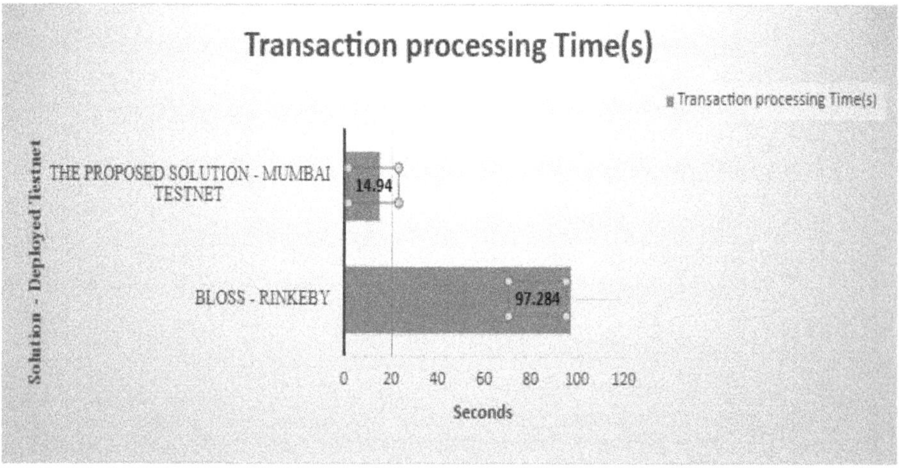

Figure: 6.15. Comparative Analysis of Transaction Processing Timing

6.2.4. Easy to deploy

The proposed solution deployed over Polygon's official TestNet – Mumbai TestNet to facilitates collaboration between various heterogeneous networks. From deployment perspective, the proposed solution is easy to deploy over any network and any environment. Generally, Deployment of Collaborative solution is very tedious tasks requires additional network infrastructure, protocols and integration with existing environment. As we seen earlier some collaborative solutions such as DOTS protocols

(Bremler-Barr & Sabag, 2022) requires additional network infrastructure and comes up with integration challenges for collaborator's existing network.

On contrary, the proposed solution deployed with no additional network infrastructure and minimal integration and configuration. The collaborative mitigation scheme deployed over Polygon's Mumbai TestNet and accessible via internet. Whereas the intra-domain mitigation solution contains attack detection layer (IDS/IPS) and attack mitigation layer (firewall) requires minimal configuration and integration along with provides high level of flexibility in terms of selection of appropriate tool based on network infrastructure. This intra-domain solution basically deploys at network gateway of any collaborator's network. The proposed solution is easy to deploy and flexible compared to other collaborative solutions, after considering these details.

6.2.5. Cost effective

Cost becomes a one of the factors other than feasibility that decides adoption of any solution in real time. The proposed solution is analysed by combining the cost of Intra-domain scheme and Collaborative mitigation scheme. Firstly, in Intra-domain scheme, we utilized open-source IDS/IPS tool names Snort at attack detection layer and an IP blocking firewall by default at the attack mitigation layer. The cost of these open-source tools and its integration with existing infrastructure are significantly nominal and sometimes available without any charges. Moreover, the collaborative mitigation scheme deployed over blockchain based infrastructure, where IPFS employed for attack signature file storage that again open-source, distributed storage. Additionally, the smart contracts of the proposed solution deployed over Polygon blockchain, which is more cost-effective solution than Ethereum. The significant contribution of this research is gas optimisation to process the attack information sharing transactions over Polygon blockchain. This gas optimization is achieved through IPFS hash storage over the blockchain. So overall cost to invoke a smart contract and to process a transaction are significantly less compared to other blockchain based solutions.

In this research, we evaluated the proposed solution's performance by comparing its transmission cost with other existing blockchain based mitigation solution's transmission costs. The cost of transmission is the cost of transmitting attack information to other collaborators through smart contracts. The transmission cost is calculated by combining the costs of Gas utilization of all the functions of Smart contracts of the proposed solution. Table 6.8 shows details information about the cost calculation for the proposed solution.

Contract	**Function**	**Gas used**	**Actual cost (Matic)**	**Actual cost (ether)**	**USD**
addCollaborator	Create addCollaborator contract	299,925	0.000749813	0.00000025	0.00041
	addAddress()	66,053	0.000165133	0.000000056	0.000091
addAllHashStorage	Create addAllHashStorage Contract	420,972	0.00105243	0.00000036	0.00058
	setHash()	88,813	0.000222033	0.000000075	0.00012
addIpfsHashStorage	Create addIpfsHashStorage contract	713,159	0.001782898	0.0000006	0.00099
	setIPFSHash	136,913	0.000342283	0.00000012	0.00019
Total cost				0.000001461	0.002381

Table 6.8. Transmission cost calculation of the proposed solutionNote – Cost such as Matic, Ether and USD are calculated as per 12/2/2024

For further validation of the proposed solution in terms of transmission cost, we compared the transmission cost of the existing solution with Bloss (Rodrigues et al, 2020) and Cochain-SC (Abou El Houda et al. 2019). These two existing solutions deployed their smart contracts on the Ethereum blockchain, and in the proposed solution, we deployed contracts on Polygon Blockchain, so we converted our Matic gas cost into Ether for comparative analysis.

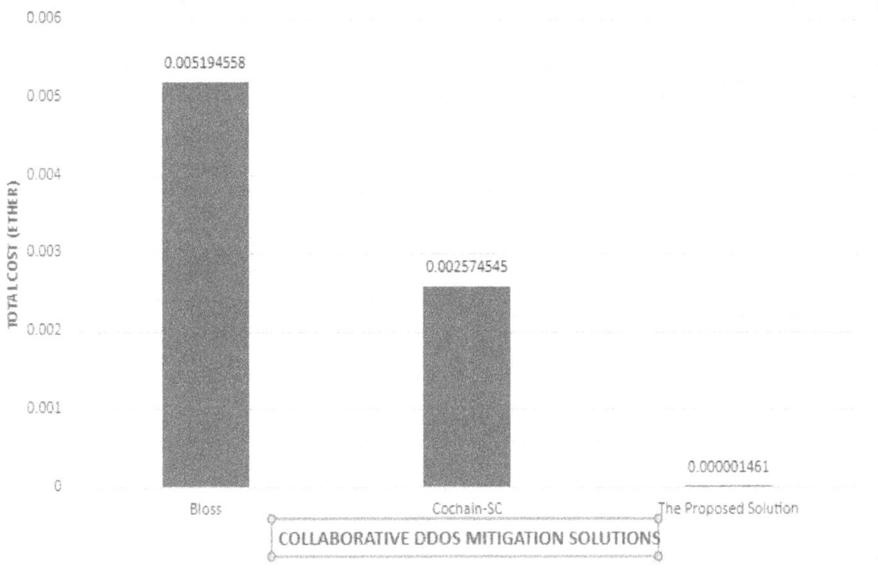

Figure: 6.16. Comparative Analysis of Transmission Cost – In Ether

The Figure. 6.16 illustrates a comparative of Transmission Cost of three Collaborative DDoS attacks mitigation solutions. This Comparative analysis provides insights about the cost comparison among the various solutions. It clearly indicates that the transmission cost of the proposed solution is negligible compared to two other solutions. Additionally, the gas optimization nature of the proposed solution directly affects to the cost effectiveness of the proposed solution.

6.2.6. Resource optimization / Energy Consumption

Resource Optimization is one of the key metrics to evaluate the performance of any system. Resource optimization generally refers to efficient utilization of computational, bandwidth, and energy resources of a network infrastructure. The proposed system used blockchain based infrastructure for collaboration among participating networks. In Blockchain Ecosystem, Resource optimization mainly relates to Energy consumption of consensus mechanism of a blockchain. Generally, Proof-of-Work blockchain consumes more energy resources than other blockchains. Additionally, Gas consumption for transaction processing also taken into consideration while choosing Proof-of-Stack blockchain.

In this research, we used Proof-of-Stack based blockchain – Polygon Blockchain to deploy a blockchain based infrastructure. Polygon is a Layer-2 solution for Ethereum, which provide high scalability, security and interoperability with Ethereum mainchain. Additionally, Gas consumption for transaction processing is also significantly low compared to Ethereum blockchain, which shows resource optimization / Energy consumption of Polygon blockchain. Moreover, in proposed solution, attack signature data stores over IPFS, not directly over Polygon blockchain, which drastically reduces Gas consumption of Smart contracts as only IPFS hashes have been written on the Polygon blockchain.

Apart from the blockchain infrastructure, the proposed solution refers lightweight IPS/IDS and utilized existing mitigation systems of collaborators networks for attack detection and mitigation, which defines optimize utilization of network resources by implementing intra-domain mitigation scheme.

6.2.7. Scalability

Scalability is one of the key performance metrics when deploying application in real environment. Scalability defines how efficiently a system handle increasing numbers of transactions, requests and users without performance degradation. As the proposed solution is built by utilizing blockchain based architecture, analysis of polygon blockchain provides clear picture about scalability of the proposed solution. According to Polygon mainnet, Polygon Proof of Stack (PoS) process 1000 or more transactions per second (TPS) which is a good amount of TPS in blockchain ecosystem (*Polygon PoS | The Most Efficient Blockchain Protocol*, n.d., 2025 & Chainspect, 2025). Additionally, while reviewing the non-functional requirement of the proposed solution, we estimated number of transactions per second would be less than 300 TPS in worse case and accordingly chose the Polygon blockchain. Additionally, Transaction Processing time (includes block creation time + Finality time) of the Polygon mainnet is around ~5 – 10 seconds, which is significantly best time in blockchain ecosystem. Moreover, the polygon blockchain (Polygon PoS) utilized sidechain as a scalability mechanism which is again among the best scalability mechanism to achieve scalability in production environment. Furthermore, Polygon blockchain (PoS) can handle millions of transactions with high throughput and low latency (*Polygon PoS | The Most Efficient Blockchain Protocol*, n.d., 2025). By considering all these factors, it is defined that the proposed solution gets high scalability as its blockchain based infrastructure utilized highly scalable Polygon Blockchain.

The proposed solution got evaluation based on various performance measures that directly indicates the proposed solution is feasible, adoptable and applicable in real time systems (networks) that intended to mitigate volumetric DDoS attacks on Collaborative manner by utilizing blockchain based infrastructure.

6.3. Conclusion and Future Directions

In conclusion, this thesis has presented a blockchain based architecture to mitigate Volumetric DDoS attacks in collaborative manner. This proposed architecture intended to provide Volumetric DDoS attacks mitigation among heterogeneous networks (collaborators) by utilizing blockchain technology. As Collaborative DDoS attacks mitigation solutions enabled various integration challenges, infrastructure complexity while implementing on an existing network. The proposed solution tried to solve this collaboration challenge by enabling blockchain technology by providing open and transparent collaboration among networks belongs to heterogeneous environments. The proposed solution contributes to sharing attacks information among collaborators by utilizing blockchain based infrastructure. The open, transparent and secure transmission of attack signature between untrusted networks efficiently is a significant offering of the proposed solution in collaborative ecosystem. As the proposed solution follows collaborative approach, repeated attack detection and mitigation tasks are significantly reduced as attack detection information already utilized through the proposed solution. This directly improves network performance and resource utilization while under-attack scenario at collaborators' end. Moreover, the proposed solution also provides attack detection and mitigation through Intra-network mitigation scheme that directly implemented on top of existing network infrastructure with minimal configurations. This intra-network scheme is closely connected through the Collaborative mitigation scheme for inter-network communication. As such, the proposed solution enables a complete mitigation solution that contains capabilities of Intra-domain as well as inter-domain to mitigate Volumetric DDoS attacks.

Moreover, The Collaborative Volumetric DDoS mitigation scheme contains blockchain based architecture that facilitates open, transparent and secure collaboration among collaborators. The blockchain based infrastructure such as Blockchain layer, Decentralized storage – IPFS,

Smart contracts, and DApps combinedly creates a collaborative mitigation scheme. The proposed solution is deployed over Polygon's official Mumbai TestNet. The Polygon blockchain provides high scalability, security and efficient transmission of attack information in distributed and transparent way to all the collaborators. As Polygon is Layer 2 solution that implemented sidechain for scalability enables high throughput and latency in transaction processing along with that it also enables the proposed solution to interoperable with Ethereum blockchain for future development. Furthermore, the proposed solution optimizes the gas cost while storing and transferring the attack information among the collaborators, which is one of the significant contributions in blockchain ecosystem. Attack signature data storage over IPFS, a decentralized storage also reduces risk of single point of failure and build transparency and trust among participating networks. By sharing this attack information among collaborators also become helpful in blocking of detected attack near the source of attack, means blocked attack traffic will not transmit to other domains as it already blocked by the source domain through Intra-network mitigation scheme.

Apart from Collaborative mitigation scheme of the proposed solution, the Intra-network volumetric DDoS attack scheme equally provides volumetric DDoS attacks detection and mitigation within a collaborators' networks. We designed this Intra-domain mitigation scheme in such a way that it provides high flexibility in selection of detection and mitigation tools and strategies to the participating networks (Collaborators) so efficient and flexible attack detection and mitigation has been performed according to individual network infrastructure and mitigation strategy. This flexibility brings more openness and participation in the proposed system collaboration as individual network is independent on selection of their mitigation strategies and tools while participating in the collaborative attack mitigation. Additionally, the Intra-network mitigation scheme also enhances the attack detection and mitigation capability by utilizing already detected attack information for future attack detection (at collaborator's network) through integrating with collaborative mitigation scheme. This strategy also becomes helpful not only for detection of volumetric DDoS attack but also reduces the risk of various IP based cyber-attacks.

The proposed solution has been evaluated by testing it over various network environment such as Controlled environment, distributed network and real time environment. By evaluating the results of these experiments, it is it stated that the proposed solution is completely blocked the Volumetric DDoS attacks (TCP, UDP and ICMP flood) on collaborators' environment. To validate the proposed solution with existing research studies and real time system matrices, we evaluated the proposed solution using various performance matrices. From this performance Evalution results, we can say that the proposed solution provides high mitigation effectiveness as outbound traffic were observed 27 times low after enabling the proposed solution over collaborator's system (on real environment). Additionally, the proposed solution took less transaction processing time 14.94 s compared to other blockchain based attack mitigation solution. Furthermore, cost effective and gas optimized solution compared to other Collaborative solutions by only 0.000001461 Ether total transmission cost. Additionally, the proposed solution provides high security, scalability and resource optimization, by utilizing blockchain based architecture and meets criteria of real-time solutions.

This research provides a valuable contribution towards interdisciplinary area of blockchain technology and cyber security. But in this research area, many domains are still unexplored and undiscovered. The proposed research would also be applicable to other IP related attacks mitigation such as spamming attacks, port scanning and Man-in-the-Middle Relay Attempts. Apart from that, this research would also provide great insights to the logging and monitoring of sensitive applications by enabling secure, reliable and transparent transmission and storage of network logs, traces in decentralized manner.

www.ingramcontent.com/pod-product-compliance
Lightning Source LLC
LaVergne TN
LVHW051922051126
851857LV00021B/2107
9798240808371